SIMPLY HUMAN

REFLECTIONS ON THE LIFE WE SHARE

SIMPLY HUMAN

REFLECTIONS ON THE LIFE WE SHARE

ALAN BODNAR, PhD

For Dayle, my partner in all things.

"I am a part of all that I have met."
—Alfred Lord Tennyson, *Ulysses*

CONTENTS

ACKNOWLEDGMENTS

As one of my patients once observed, his life is the product of many people. The same can be said of this book, and I want to thank them all. My gratitude begins at home to my wife, Dayle, and children, Christine and Matthew. They are the reason and inspiration for all that I do and my first creative team, helping to bring this book into the world. My thanks go to Dayle for her unwavering support, to Christine whose love of reading inspires me to write, and to Matthew and his wife Jessica for their encouragement and consultation about the practical issues of book design.

In my professional life as a psychologist, I have been fortunate to share my journey with mentors, colleagues, students, and patients who have instructed, encouraged, challenged, inspired, and enriched me with their knowledge, wisdom, humor, and generosity of spirit in allowing me to become part of their own stories. Their mark is on every one of the essays in this collection, and I hope I have managed to convey some idea of the richness of their contributions.

I am grateful also to Doctor Denise Yocum, the founding publisher of *Massachusetts Psychologist* and *New England Psychologist*, for giving me the opportunity to share my thoughts about anything and everything in the monthly "In Person" column since 1993 and for permission to reprint these columns for this book.

I thank my readers for their company as I imagine writing to friends I know and those I will never meet. I am indebted to Dan Wakefield, my writing mentor, for the example of his own work, his belief in me as a writer, and for his encouragement and practical advice about publishing. My thanks go also to Peggy Payne, my literary consultant, to fellow writer Keith Yocum for his advice and encouragement, to Susan Gonsalves, my longtime editor, and to David Ter-Avanesyan for his amazing work in designing this book.

I am privileged to have a great group of friends, old and new, and I thank them all for the good company, hearty laughs, lively conversations, and mutual support that we share. I appreciate their time, their willingness to share their opinions, and their patience in helping me with some of the many decisions involved in producing this book. To some of my oldest friends, the guys in the Middlesex County Philosophical Association, dedicated to shooting hoops and the breeze, thanks for being there through all these years.

INTRODUCTION

When I answered the phone one day in early March of 1993, Dr. Denise Yocum introduced herself as the publisher of *Massachusetts* Psychologist, a monthly newspaper distributed to licensed psychologists living in Massachusetts and New York.

She said she was calling because she read an essay that I had written for the newsletter of the Massachusetts Psychological Association and was inviting me to write a column for her new publication. We called the column "In Person" to capture its function of providing a window into the experiences of a psychologist as he went about his life and work.

I began writing in this way a few years earlier with the publication of the essay that captured Dr. Yocum's attention. It was a piece about the widespread effects of the state's closing or privatizing of hospitals and outpatient mental health clinics.

My aim in that essay was to go behind the headlines and show how these decisions were affecting real people, people who had lost their presence and voice in the world through years of struggling with mental illnesses that had shunted them into obscurity.

I wanted to convey some of the fear, confusion, and betrayal that these people were feeling and, in some small way, give voice to the distress that policymakers appeared to be ignoring. I suppose I thought that if people knew how it felt to lose vital services, they would find a way to work for a more just and compassionate mental health care system.

The chance to write the "In Person" column gave me the opportunity to continue describing the daily lives and struggles of people with mental illness who were being treated in outpatient clinics and state hospitals.

My own career as a clinical psychologist brought me first to the inner city of Boston where I worked with children and families in outpatient clinics and then to a series of four state hospitals for the treatment of children and adults with severe and persistent mental illnesses.

When I began writing the column in 1993, I had been working at Westborough State Hospital in Westborough, Massachusetts, for about six months.

Westborough closed in 2010, and I accepted a position at Worcester State Hospital, where I worked until that facility was replaced by the Worcester Recovery Center and Hospital in 2012.

I retired in 2015 but continue to share a psychologist's view of everyday life in *New England Psychologist*, the new name under which *Massachusetts Psychologist* has been published and distributed to a regional audience since 2002.

What began as an attempt to describe the lives of people who most consider very different quickly turned into an examination of our similarities. As I wrote about the sadness of people who lost much of their lives to chronic mental illness, I connected with my own experiences of loss and sadness.

Similarly, I found a common bond with my patients in our individually unique but nevertheless universal experiences of joy, uncertainty, anxiety, and all the other emotions that animate the human heart.

The people I write about are our friends, neighbors, relatives, the wealthy and the poor, some who have achieved and lost much, and others who never had a chance. To protect their privacy, I have disguised their identities by not using their real names and changing the circumstances but not the substance of the challenges that brought us together.

This collection of 66 essays, selected from the 258 pieces I wrote between March of 1993 and July of 2016, focuses on the common human experiences that unite us all regardless of the state of our mental health or our positions in society.

Empathy, loss, change, sadness, integrity, community, the ways we manage stress, and the idea of life as story are all part of the human equation. They are the stars of these stories that I have been telling for more than two decades as I have been going about my life and work.

For this collection, I selected columns that I especially enjoyed writing, stories that still moved me as they had when I first wrote them, and that I thought would have the widest appeal.

I found that these sixty-six pieces comprised ten different themes, each of which became the basis for one of the ten chapters of the collection. As a group, these ten chapters of little stories tell the bigger story of how I discovered what has been most important to me in my work and life—the centrality of our connection to one another, born in empathy, nurtured by the awareness of our common struggles, given form in community, and passed on to the next generation.

Although this is not memoir in the traditional sense, I have included some autobiographical material in an introduction to each chapter. By doing so, I hope to provide the reader with enough insight into the "person" of me, the writer, to gain a better understanding of my influences and biases and to show "backstage" a psychologist at work.

These essays are not meant exclusively for psychologists. While psychologists may identify more readily with the descriptions of psychological work with people struggling with severe and persistent mental illness, I hope that any reader will gain a new appreciation for the very human dimensions of illness and the journey of recovery. Whether we are mentally well or mentally ill, we are all much more alike than different or, as twentieth-century psychiatrist Harry Stack Sullivan put it, "simply human." Regardless of who we are and how we spend our days, we are united by the bond of our shared humanity as we try to live our lives the best we can.

Alan Bodnar, Ph.D.
Wellesley, Massachusetts

ONE

EMPATHY

The story begins with empathy, the ability to put ourselves in another person's shoes and to experience the world from a perspective other than our own. Unless we have this capacity, there is little hope of understanding and none of community.

Without empathy, we go through our lives as so many solitudes glancing off one another as we remain locked in the prisons of our personal concerns. Empathy comes with the recognition that we are all more alike than different, and the stories in this chapter describe some of these similarities. Love and longing, fear and grief, the impulse to question unjust fate, fear of mortality and change, humiliation and anger are just some of the universal movements of the heart that make empathy and understanding possible.

With empathy comes the realization that we are all ordinary heroes muddling through life with as much grace and courage as we can muster.

The essays in this chapter span a period of twenty-three years between 1993 and 2015, roughly corresponding to the time I worked at Westborough State Hospital and then at the Worcester Recovery Center and Hospital with people facing the challenges of major mental illness including schizophrenia, major depression, and bipolar disorder.

The first fifteen years of my professional career between 1975 and 1990 were devoted to work with children and families in outpatient clinics, and the first essay, "The Boy on the Bike and Other Ordinary Heroes," draws on my experience doing home visits to families in Boston.

In the twenty-three years covered by these essays, my wife and I have had our share of joys and sorrows. We saw our two children grow to young adulthood while we suffered the loss of my father in 1996 and my wife's father and my mother in 2005.

After four strokes left him progressively weaker throughout his seventies, my father died at the age of eighty. He was a quiet and gentle man who worked in a factory that made boilers for oceangoing vessels. When the company left town, he was hired by the county road department where he painted traffic signs, none better than the Sesame Street sign he made for his grandchildren.

In the way he lived his life, he modeled humility, and I'm sure that if he had ever had what Rudyard Kipling described as the opportunity to "walk with kings," he would have done so without ever losing the "common touch." My journey through my father's illness and death taught me about loss and grief, bringing me closer to the men and women whose mental illnesses made loss their constant companion.

Does empathy give us the common touch, or is it the other way around? Either way, there is a close and mutually reinforcing relationship between the two. If I can take the trouble to look at the world from another's perspective, then my understanding and empathy for that person will surely increase. Yet we may need a certain amount of empathy from the beginning to motivate us to take that perspective in the first place.

Empathy is far more than the ability to identify with loss and sorrow. It is a quality of perception that looks beyond obvious differences among people to the essence of what it means to be human in the full array of thoughts, feelings, and reactions to life's triumphs and tragedies. When we look beyond our differences, we find the common human center.

The essays in this chapter tell the stories of people widely separated by geography, mental functioning, socioeconomic status, nationality, and social roles, yet by the simple acts of imagination and memory, we can see ourselves in their circumstances.

A grandmother makes a home for her neglected grandchildren. A patient prepares for the death of his best friend. Wounded pride brings two men to blows on a train. Life changes in an instant for the victims of a tsunami on the shores of the Indian Ocean.

Sometimes empathy requires us to go beyond recognition of the obvious and to imagine an unknown dimension of another's life. "Imagining Pittsburgh" describes the efforts of members of a therapy group to imagine the life of a group leader leaving to go back to his hometown at the end of his internship year.

In that same essay, we hear the voice of a man about to be discharged from the hospital. While he is happy to be moving on, he has bigger dreams than the plans we made for him. It makes us wonder if we had done enough to imagine him succeeding in a bigger arena and helped him prepare to try.

In the summer of 2010, my wife and I took our second cross-country train trip, leaving from a suburban Boston station and arriving in Seattle four days later after a stopover in Montana's Glacier National Park. We traveled in coach, avoiding the expense of a sleeper car to get what rest we could in our reclining seats. Everybody has a story to tell on a train, and the essay "Ambushed by Insight" describes how sharing stories and the adventures of travel with strangers builds empathy and brings people closer together.

I retired from full-time work as a clinical psychologist in June of 2015 after agonizing over the decision for many months. The columns I wrote during these months clearly reflect my concerns about growing old, losing my sense of purpose, and becoming irrelevant.

I am discovering that the emotional work of these years provides an opportunity to draw closer to people marginalized by age, illness, poverty, and social disadvantages. One group with which I am becoming increasingly familiar is that of people with dementia living in memory care centers and nursing homes. References to their plight appear later in this chapter and throughout the book.

My mother died of complications of Alzheimer's disease in 2005 in a comfortable, caring facility just minutes from my home. Getting her there was a different story involving years of managing her care in New Jersey from my home in Massachusetts because she refused to leave her apartment.

Now we are caring for another family member, an otherwise healthy centenarian with an unspecified dementia, currently living in a specialized facility about thirty minutes away from us—just a short trip but a long, sad journey.

Everything we experience in life is an opportunity and a challenge to develop empathy, to realize that we are more alike than different, and to draw closer together. And so, the story begins.

The Boy on the Bike and Other Ordinary Heroes

In the streets of the city, you might see Jimmy flying by on his bicycle, standing on the pedals, moving too fast to sit. He leans forward into the breeze that ruffles the thin material of his oversized white T-shirt. At seven, Jimmy is an active boy with a good mind, an agile body, and a past filled with too much violence and unpredictability.

Jimmy's kindergarten teacher introduced me to him two years earlier because she was frustrated by his defiance of authority and worried about his frequent talk about wanting to join his uncle in heaven. To say that his traumatic history was consistent with his problems in the classroom may be intellectually satisfying, but it neglects the heartrending emotional impact of his story.

No one survives the terror and insecurity that Jimmy experienced without determination and resilience. Jimmy and his grandmother Ruth had both in abundance.

Jimmy was born to an alcoholic and drug-addicted teenage girl whose penchant for larceny and assault led her in and out of jail. When she was indisposed, she left her son with friends, or with her own mother, or with no one.

Even more than most children in this all too common situation, Jimmy grew up fast. At the age of two, he once got up after midnight and, not finding his mother at home, left the apartment and walked across the street and into the bar looking for her. Mother felt bad, so she bought her Jimmy a two-wheeler. The new bike had no training wheels, so it sat unused until Jimmy learned to ride it by himself as a three-year-old.

Life might have gone on this way for Jimmy had his mother not incurred the anger of a local drug dealer. Running for her life, she took her son West to the safety of the boy's great grandparent's farm. It was there that Jimmy met his great uncle Paul, a kindly old man who had long ago lost his arm in a mishap with a harvesting machine. His accident had never stopped Uncle Paul from fishing, and now he took Jimmy with him. For a brief period of time, Jimmy had the space and freedom to be just a kid.

The following year when word came east that Uncle Paul had died, Jimmy began talking about wanting to join him in heaven.

If ever a story needed a hero, it was now, and Jimmy's grandmother Ruth stepped forward to fill the role admirably.

She moved to a safer apartment and brought Jimmy and his then two-year-old sister to live with her. Ruth put both of them in a good nursery school and recruited two of her most responsible children to help with babysitting in return for room and board.

Somehow, she managed to hold down two jobs, to respond to the children's need for time and attention, to handle the family crises that were always erupting, and to meet with me, the therapist who presumed to help this family.

Every week, I made my way to the side street of identical brick houses where Ruth lived with the children. The tired swing on her small porch where she could watch the world go by got little use except as a beacon for awkward strangers.

And, though we soon stopped being strangers, the feeling of awkwardness never entirely left me as I sat in the eternal summer of Ruth's plant-filled living room in the presence of more sorrow and strength than many people experience in a lifetime.

If the effectiveness of psychotherapy depended on the charisma or life experience of the therapist, then we would have little to show for our efforts. When I was a twenty-three-year-old intern nervously awaiting the arrival of one of my first patients—an attorney twice my age—I wondered what I could possibly offer to a man who had seen so much of life.

My supervisor assured me that all I needed to begin was an understanding of the conceptual tools and techniques of our trade and a willingness to learn from the patient.

In the same way, I tried to learn from Jimmy and Ruth as I saw the boy each week in my office and his grandmother at home. In their company, I was standing at the meeting point of enormous forces of personal history, present demands, and individual courage and determination. My vantage point felt as precarious as the outcropping of rock where I once stood to admire the confluence of the Potomac and Shenandoah Rivers, and the human energy generated by this family seemed every bit as powerful.

Perhaps I played a small part in clearing a branch from a trickle here and there, nurturing a rivulet or two of new perspectives on old challenges. All the while, the torrent surged around me, but above its roar, a quiet message hung in the air like the spray that lingers whenever currents collide.

It is the message that all of our patients offer as a gift, as a prayer, as a whispered reminder that we are all heroes together, ordinary people burdened with misfortune and struggling in obscurity to live our lives as fully and decently as we can.

From *Massachusetts Psychologist*, May 1993.

MY FATHER'S SURGEON

When I was a kid, I used to think that doctors never got sick, teachers never had to struggle to learn anything, and the clergy had a direct connection to God. I had no preconceived notions about psychologists because I had never met one, but if I had, I suppose I would have imagined that he or she could always be counted on to be calm, cool, and rational.

The years have taught me that doctors sicken, teachers forget, and the clergy stumble around in the dark like the rest of us. As for psychologists, I only wonder if our patients see us as the untroubled, emotionless, blank screens that we so often try to be for their sakes.

I wonder this as I sit alone in my office with the door closed waiting for a telephone call from my father's surgeon, 250 miles away. A conference can be left early, lunch can wait, but in forty-five minutes, the door will be opened again to admit the afternoon's first patient.

Meanwhile, I sit and wait for the phone to bring me a chance to talk to the stranger my father may allow to cut into his fragile arteries.

I try to catch up on my paperwork. There are always reports to write and so I begin, "The patient is an alert, oriented, middle-aged man who has become depressed and anxious about his parents' declining health."

I wonder if I am writing about the patient or me, the therapist, so I put the report aside for now and review the list of questions I have prepared for my father's surgeon.

How do you interview a man for the job of taking responsibility for the life of your own father? I will ask him about the risks and benefits of surgery, hoping that they can be put into numbers, as if this situation involved a simple decision about where to invest money.

What is an acceptable level of risk when a failure rate of even one in one hundred is too high if the failure is the man who has always been your emotional anchor?

All I know about the surgeon is that my parents were favorably impressed by his open, confident manner, that his card advertises him as a diplomate in his specialty, that he has a Mediterranean-sounding name.

I turn that name over in my mind, listening to the rhythm of its syllables as I would listen to a line of poetry. I imagine his voice, deep, heavily accented, and serious. How could a surgeon be anything but serious, challenging mortality every day, cutting into the very center of human life with little room for error?

I have often tried to comfort students who are panicked over a mistake in therapy with the thought that psychotherapy is more forgiving than brain surgery, but today I want the precision of the surgeon and warmth of the therapist embodied in one man at the other end of the telephone line. I really want guaranteed success, perfect health for my father, and a pledge that we will all live forever. I want the impossible, but I'll settle for a competent professional, a good man doing his best.

I use the telephone every day, but now I suddenly look at it with the same mixture of hope and dread that I felt four years ago when it connected me to another team of doctors keeping me informed of my father's condition after I left his side following major surgery and a third stroke.

As his condition sharply deteriorated and then slowly improved, his own voice registered his gradually returning strength. What I know of Resurrection comes from a curious combination of the Church and the telephone company.

I try to read and am pleasantly surprised when an engaging article about schizophrenia by a colleague across the hall captures my attention. At last the phone rings, and a woman's voice says that the doctor can speak with me now. There follows a silence that is quickly broken by the friendly, energetic, almost cheerful voice of the surgeon.

There is talk of risks and benefits, even percentages, together with an arcane description of the long and convoluted journey of blood to the brain. The surgeon has done this procedure many times before and speaks with confidence and compassion. There is so much information to absorb, but there will be time for that later. Working on pure emotion, I am encouraged by our conversation, and no sooner do I say thank you and goodbye, than I hear my first patient of the afternoon knocking on the door.

The young man enters the room and nervously sits in the chair opposite mine. "I am scared," he begins. "Yes, of course," I reply, "Please go on."

Adapted from *Massachusetts Psychologist*, June 1993.

•••

MY FATHER'S VOICE

When my father died this spring, there were no deathbed speeches or last words of wisdom. His evenhanded kindness and respect for everyone were enough to tell me that we are all more alike than different.

I see the truth of this lesson every day at the hospital, but never more clearly than when death interrupts our routines and levels the usual distinctions between doctors and patients, professionals and laborers, the psychotic and the sane.

Six months ago, one of our patients committed suicide. As I knelt shoulder to shoulder with other professionals and patients in a crowded auditorium at his memorial Mass, I felt a sense of community and fellowship unlike anything I had experienced in the hospital until then. I would not have dared to predict that my father's death, only three months later, would bring this feeling back but with greater intensity and personal meaning.

But now I am sitting with our clinical team in a small room on the second floor of a wood frame building, one of our hospital's quarter-way houses. The name comes from the assumption that the journey from the locked units to this place comprises twenty-five percent of the way back to the community, the way back from the torments of psychosis to the world of the safe and sane.

We are meeting to review the progress of Gordon, a young man with a long history of schizophrenia and alcohol addiction and, most recently, depression triggered by the terminal illness of his best friend, Edward.

The tall, slender man enters the room and slowly folds himself, like a stiff-jointed carpenter's ruler, into a waiting armchair. "I don't feel bad for Edward," he says, "Soon he will be in heaven where he will be happy forever."

The words of an ancient prayer come to me, "Eternal rest grant unto him, O Lord." I have been saying this prayer since I was a boy, for grandparents, aunts, uncles, cousins, strangers I read about in the newspapers. Soon I will say it for Edward, but now, above all, it is a prayer for my father.

Yet it is hard to think of my father as needing this kind of petition. He was a humble man who always put others first. When we crowded into his hospital room, he moved his oxygen mask aside to tell us where we could find another chair so everyone could be comfortable. I find it easier to pray to him than for him. Like Gordon anticipating the fate of his best friend, I cannot feel badly for my father. He is surely in heaven where he is happy.

Someone hastens to remind Gordon that Edward's death will be a terrible loss for him, that he will feel very sad. "I don't feel sad," Gordon replies, "just cold." What kind of cold, I want to ask. Is it the cold of the wind howling through the middle of your stomach?

I first knew that icy, hollow chill when I realized my father was dying. Even now it may be quietly waiting to ambush me when I come out from behind the cover of my work, my family, and my friends. If I should suddenly stop, look around and appear puzzled, perhaps I am only wondering if others can hear the rushing wind.

"But," says Gordon, "I am afraid that I will be weak when Edward dies because the people who love us make us stronger." Yes Gordon, Edward strengthened you with his support, his friendship, the many things he did for you and taught you to do for yourself. All this will be missing from your life when he is gone.

Still, there is a way to keep Edward's spirit alive, a way that his death can keep you strong. Think about what you admired about Edward and try to develop these qualities in yourself. That can be his lasting gift to you.

My father's death was not unexpected, although the precise moment of death always comes as a surprise. For a long time, but especially in the last month of his life, I had been imagining that, before he died, my father would tell me to listen carefully, to pay attention, that he was only going to say this once. Then he would impart to me some great wisdom, the secret of life, or at least a last request. One day as I sat at the side of his bed and caught sight of him looking pensive, I asked what he was thinking. He replied, "What are *you* thinking?"

Did I really imagine that this man of few words and kind deeds would be anything but consistent, that he would speak with the tongues of angels at the hour of his death? Did I really imagine that I needed anything more than the example of his life? Be considerate of others, bear suffering with courage, grace, and good humor, get used to loneliness. Did I really think I needed the words to make me strong?

Gordon leaves the interview with the team's approval and encouragement to continue visiting his friend at the hospice. For months, we have seen each other coming and going from this house, one quarter of the way to sanity. He calls me "Doc" and thinks that my world is nothing like his, but now another voice from somewhere deep within, my father's voice, reminds me it isn't so.

From *Massachusetts Psychologist*, July 1996.

• • •

MUDDLING THROUGH TOGETHER

My friend Jack has the best reply I've ever heard to the polite question of "how are you?" "Muddling through," he says with a wry smile and a twinkle in his eye. The questioner always smiles back and, if my own reaction is in any way typical, leaves not only understanding Jack but also feeling understood himself. When you come right down to it, there's no more honest description of the human condition—Jack's, mine, and yours—than "muddling through."

Consider the alternatives. "Fine thanks, and you?" is the gold standard of brief social exchange, and I am not for a moment advocating its replacement. It is particularly suitable for brief encounters as we hurry past one another on stairways or cross paths in parking lots, especially when we do not know one another very well. And, as far as it goes, the answer is true enough. We are all, in fact, "fine," or, in other words, things could always be worse.

One of my patients is in the habit of answering the ordinary social inquiry about his well-being with a carefully rehearsed string of superlatives, "terrific, fantastic, super, excellent," emphasizing each word by pounding his hand on an imaginary podium.

Another twenty minutes in his presence gives the lie to his overly enthusiastic description of his mood. He is as tormented as ever about his dilemma of languishing in the safe and familiar environment of the hospital or taking the risk of trying and possibly failing in the community.

Of course, the other alternative is to emphasize the negative, as in, "How are you?"—"Lousy." I wouldn't recommend this on a busy stairway or in a crowded elevator, though if your listener is sympathetic and you both have the time and interest to explore the issue, it can be a perfectly honest response.

The main problem with "fantastic" and "lousy" is that, presuming they are not the products of distortion or manipulation, they are still exaggerations. When we give either answer, we are seizing and magnifying the feeling of the moment and, in so doing, neglecting the larger context of our lives.

Ralph has been in the hospital almost continuously for more than twenty-five years, and for much of that time, an objective observer would be perfectly accurate in saying that he was doing "lousy." Ralph's particular version of lousy included sitting in a corner by himself with a forlorn expression on his face, skipping off hospital grounds to the nearest bar to drown whatever was left of his reason and judgment in a fifth of whiskey, and every now and then, assaulting a staff member who reminded him a little too much of an abusive uncle.

Now Ralph is a veteran of the system or what he would call an accomplished mental patient. It had taken him over a quarter century to achieve his status as elder statesman, but just when he did, something happened to make Ralph wonder if there might not be a different and better life for him in the community.

An alert intern caught the meaning of his quiet muttering one day in a group session, and now, three years later, Ralph is living on an unlocked unit in the hospital, working part-time in town, and preparing for discharge.

Some might call Ralph's transformation a miracle, a miracle of better medicines, internalized structure, maturation, or simply the passage of time. No one would doubt that he has gone from doing "lousy" to doing "terrific;" no one, that is, except maybe Ralph himself.

When I listen to Ralph these days, I hear a man burdened with fear and doubt, doing well in all the usual ways we measure progress, but not feeling as terrific as he looks.

An introspective man, Ralph looks back on his life with a set of theories about what led to his troubles. He looks back on his troubles with gratitude for the care he received and remorse for the hurt he caused others. But when Ralph looks forward, he does so with a combination of determination and uncertainty. He looks ahead to a life of what my friend Jack would call "muddling through." In fact, Ralph has the wisdom to realize that this is exactly what he has been doing all along.

Perhaps the essence of mental health is the ability to recognize that we spend our days "muddling through" life, neither "flying high" with all of the answers nor "bogging down" in the mire of ignorance, fear, and despair.

The late Boston psychoanalyst Elvin Semrad used to say that self-deception is the only mental illness and that people deceive themselves about only two things, loss and failure. While we can fault this formulation for neglecting the biology of mental illness, it is hard to argue with its wisdom as a guide for living. To recognize and accept our losses and failures even as we celebrate our triumphs and endure our struggles is to realize with Jack and Ralph and Elvin the ordinary miracle of muddling through, and to know that in this journey, we are not alone.

From *Massachusetts Psychologist*, October 1993.

• • •

PRIDE AND HUMILIATION
THEN AND NOW

On a cold night in Connecticut, psychology caught up with me and interrupted my vacation somewhere on a railway line between Bridgeport and Waterbury. My ticket entitled me only to passage through some forty miles of New England countryside but delivered the bonus of a surprising lesson in the prevalence and power of humiliation in everyday life.

When I boarded the train with my family in Bridgeport, my attention was quickly drawn to a well-dressed man slumped in his seat, mumbling to himself and glowering at everyone entering his car.

Instinctively, we left two empty seats between the mumbler and ourselves. Before long, my wife and daughter had stretched out to rest or read in separate seats while I amused my five-year-old son with the kinds of child therapy drawing games that might have instantly blown my cover as a weary, theater-going tourist.

As the train sped on through the night, our traveling companion continued to mumble, castigating four mostly silent women for keeping him awake with their chatter. He reasoned that the railroad would not permit them to bother him if he had not been a member of a minority group. Whatever the state of this man's reality testing, his pride had obviously been wounded long before he boarded the train by the kinds of humiliations that our society doles out regularly to its minorities.

When the train pulled into the man's station and he got up to leave, another traveler, who had been sitting across the aisle and several rows behind him, inexplicably took the mumbler's seat.

The first man stared menacingly at the invader of his abandoned territory and ordered him to go. Each man sized up the other, each demanding to know where the other was from. The mumbler mockingly feigned terror when the newcomer said he was from New York, and in quick succession, there followed a challenge to settle the matter in the parking lot, a flurry of insults, and a move by the second man to pull what he said was a gun from his gym bag.

As he bent to the task, the mumbler was on him, and the two of them started throwing each other around the car.

How lucky for all involved that there was a psychologist on the train. While I wondered how I could initiate an emergency procedure we call a Code Green in the hospital, the instinct for self-preservation took over.

At that point, I shepherded my family to the back of the car where another passenger pulled the emergency brake. In addition to preventing the train from leaving the station, this act summoned a surprisingly calm conductor who ejected the mumbler and then satisfied himself that his opponent was bluffing about the gun.

Out of danger now, I felt a rising tide of anger at these two characters whose wounded pride had threatened our safety. The feeling was not unlike what I had experienced long ago in a vastly different context when I watched my much-admired President Kennedy on national television delivering an ultimatum to Soviet Premier Khrushchev during the Cuban missile crisis.

With little appreciation for the nuances or long-term consequences of global politics, I simply saw two men playing chicken with thermonuclear dragsters on Main Street. As I huddled with my high school classmates in the basement of the school cafeteria where our principal hoped sacks of Pillsbury's Best flour would shield us from danger, I cursed the pride of the world leaders who would see to it that none of us lived to finish our sophomore year.

My thoughts about the fighters on the train echoed my adolescent ideas about the President and the Premier. How could these men be so quick to strike out in anger and risk innocent lives in the name of wounded pride? I certainly would not be so foolhardy. I spent the week following the railway incident with my wife and children visiting relatives and friends, and by the time we were back home, too many dashed though foolish expectations of others left me irritable and grumpy.

In this mood, I settled down at my desk to catch up with some reading, beginning with two articles by Donald C. Klein on the subject of the "humiliation dynamic." The dynamics of humiliation, Klein tells us, are universal, and when a valued aspect of the self is subject to real or even imagined disparagement by others, we are tempted to react in anger.

The process is the same whether it occurs between neighbors or nations. While my own self-concept would never demand that I fight to protect a seat on a nearly empty train car, my personal myths may be even sillier and equally likely to provoke a different form of anger when they are not believed. And so I take my place beside the mumbler and the president, leaving plenty of room for us all.

Adapted from *Massachusetts Psychologist*, March 1994.

•••

IMAGINING PITTSBURGH

Sometimes imagination is the best guide to reality. The patients in one of our groups made this clear as our intern Mike was getting ready to leave the group at the end of the year. Mike had been preparing them for his departure for several weeks, but it was only on his last day in the group that someone asked where he was going.

His reply that he was going home to Pittsburgh pried loose from one of the men a cascade of associations. In his deep, rumbling voice now with a hint of glee, the man recited a list of loosely connected words and phrases: Pittsburgh Steelers but no NBA team, Cincinnati Royals, near Pittsburgh, a team in the old ABA. They had, what was his name? Oscar Robertson. The Cleveland Cavaliers, the Pittsburgh Pirates.

And now a question for Mike, "Do you live on a street?" We must have looked puzzled, so the man added, "or an avenue?" He wanted to know if it was near Main Street. The questioner had never been to Pittsburgh, but it is a safe bet that every burg has a Main Street somewhere.

A pause in the dialogue, a short space of silence, and another man, looking as always like he had just awakened from a trance, pipes in, "Pittsburgh? What state is that in?"

And so the session passed with more questions, comments and associations. The group members seemed to be trying to connect with Mike, to imagine him in his own setting, his own reality.

He had been here for them in this sunny room in a state hospital every Thursday for the past year, but that was about to change. By returning to Pittsburgh, Mike was emerging as a person with a life of his own, separate from their lives, distant and apart from the only place they had ever known him.

I could think only of schoolchildren, dumbstruck at the sight of their teacher in a supermarket. They wonder if it's really Ms. Jones, and if it is, what is she doing here? Doesn't she live in the school? Surely she has no need to shop and cook and eat like ordinary people, like their parents, like them.

I think of schoolchildren, but there is a difference here. Unlike the kids in the supermarket, the men and women in this therapy group are not surprised when Mike turns up in an unfamiliar setting. They do not stand in open-mouthed awe when they find him where they do not expect him to be. On the contrary, they rush to be with him where he is going. Mike is off to Pittsburgh, and on the wings of their imaginations, his patients fly off to meet him in the reality of his life.

As I watch the drama of this parting unfold, I wonder if our group members have discovered a clever strategy for never having to say goodbye or if this is a mature realization that their therapist's life is separate from theirs. Whatever their motivation, these men and women are also reminding us that their lives are separate from ours and that the reality of our therapy rooms is not the reality they live and breathe every day.

In my early days as a therapist, I worked for an agency that stressed the importance of making home visits to the children and families we served. Because the agency happened to be in one of a big city's poorer and more dangerous neighborhoods, we never knew what to expect when we reached our destination and knocked on the door.

What I remember most about those visits was the contrast in the best of situations between the evidence of violence in the streets and at least some small measure of safety that parents or grandparents, most often without the help of a partner, were trying to provide for the children in their care.

Sometimes it was a triple lock on a door, once it was a living room carefully made off-limits after a bullet shattered a window. Without those visits, our imaginations would have had to work overtime to understand the reality of the children who came to the clinic because they were failing in school, having nightmares, fighting with peers, or were simply too frightened to leave the side of someone they could trust.

And without our understanding that reality, our therapy room stocked with toys, our professional time and attention, and our poor, well-intentioned words would have added up to little more than a brief respite from life in a war zone. In later years, there were also opportunities to visit the homes of the wealthy, the privileged, and those in between, and each visit had something important to teach about the real lives of the people who lived there.

When it comes to understanding the real lives of real people, practitioners of community mental health have a particular advantage. When you work in the community you serve, walk the same streets, eat at the same lunch counters, read the same newspapers, and struggle with the same politicians as your patients do, then you hardly need to be reminded to be relevant. The rest of us need our imaginations more than ever.

The other day I sat in my office with a man who has been depressed most of his life. He is ready to leave the hospital now, impatient to be moving on, and not especially enthusiastic about the plans we have made for him. He has bigger dreams and richer memories than those of us who know him only as a hospital patient can readily imagine.

He begins to talk about the successful business he once operated in a distant city, and the faint beginnings of a smile crack the mask of his sadness. He tells me that he is much more than the depressed soul we see in the hospital. His words are a gentle challenge to imagine the Pittsburgh of the larger life that is his real home.

From *New England Psychologist*, August/September 2003.

• • •

WORLDS APART

There are worlds within worlds, and the one we call home can change in a heartbeat. This was likely the experience of the hundreds of thousands of people killed or otherwise affected by the tsunamis that scoured the shores of the Indian Ocean last December.

One minute you are sunbathing on the beach, tending your garden, or preparing dinner for your family, and the next, you are clinging to the trunk of a palm tree as a wall of muddy water breaks over you and retreats with the debris of what just a few minutes earlier had been your life.

During these times, even those of us on the other side of the world are shaken into an awareness that the differences that insulate and protect us from catastrophe are the thinnest of illusions. Life rears up and gives us a crash course in empathy.

Complacency and inertia keep us stuck in the world we know best. It makes no difference if that world is a transient state of mind or fortune in our own changing lives or the more or less stable circumstances that define each of us as unique individuals.

As for our own changing circumstances, we know that when life is going our way, it is difficult to imagine serious misfortune. In the same way, when we are down, it is hard to believe that we will ever again be cheerful and optimistic about the future. Either way, we are stuck in a state of mind that becomes a self-contained reality. Each of these worlds has its own special laws of physics and perception, affecting our experience of self, others, and the passage of time itself. Time flies when you're having fun.

Just as it is difficult to imagine life as radically different from our usual daily experience, we face an even greater challenge imagining the lives of people who typically live in worlds other than the one we inhabit. This is the challenge of empathy.

Empathy is a bridge between worlds, and whether that bridge spans the length of continents to the victims of tsunamis on the other side of the world or the length of the carpet on the therapist's floor, it marks a route that is not always easy to travel.

Sometimes we forget that we are trying to travel to worlds where the ordinary laws of physics do not apply. For the person with schizophrenia, space and time can be infinitely malleable, and so the woman her therapist accompanies to the hospital thrift shop insists on buying a size seven shoe for her size ten friend simply because it is stylish, available, and a good bargain.

Another patient, who steadfastly refuses to wear a wristwatch, is stuck on his locked ward because whenever he is permitted time by himself on hospital grounds, he does not return when he is expected. His is a long-standing and many-tiered conflict with time, the unyielding tyrant against whom he has declared open war.

Each birthday reminds him that another year has passed and he is still in the hospital with his life on hold. Laughing at the clock, he recites the same litany of ambitious dreams with little inclination to begin with more modest and attainable goals.

I see him for sixty minutes every week, but when we leave the unit, he still signs out for two hours. Just in case, he explains, something unexpected happens so we don't get in trouble for being late. We are always back in the allotted hour. He is doing much better following the schedule of my world even though he won't be bound to it on paper.

There are worlds within worlds, and connecting them with bridges of empathy can be tiring work. On one recent snowy evening after a long day, a man shuffling up the driveway called out to me as I was leaving the hospital. He was a patient with whom I had had only brief contact a long time ago.

Fairly certain that he had mistaken me for someone he knew better and too tired to make sure, I got into my car and closed the door behind me. Soon he was tapping on the window, and when I rolled it down, the man said that he was being discharged in the morning.

In my world, people do not knock on car windows to share good news with virtual strangers, though, at times, that may be exactly what we want to do. But on this snowy night, the man and I were not entirely in my world or his. We were poised on a border as thin as the window I had just rolled down, and so we simply shook hands and said goodbye.

From *New England Psychologist*, February 2005.

• • •

AMBUSHED BY INSIGHT

Metaphors abound in everyday speech, but psychologists use them mindfully, most often to clarify something that we think is important for our audience to remember. We like to think we are the masters of our metaphors, but once expressed, they have a way of doubling back and sneaking up on us with an unexpected lesson.

Setting ourselves up to be ambushed by insight, my wife and I recently boarded a westbound train in a Boston suburb and traveled to Seattle and back home again. Having done something like this trip before, we had an idea of what to expect and no illusions about having an easy or uneventful passage. We believed before we started that the concept of journey is a good metaphor for life, but that a train journey is an even better one. Here's what we learned.

- On a long train ride in coach seats, there is no privilege to rank, wealth, or social status. Even the folks in sleeping cars with the perks of beds, showers, first call to the dining car, and wine tastings still have to contend with bumpy stretches of track and long intervals of speed reduced to fifteen miles per hour because a slow freight has the right of way or flash floods threaten to wash out the rail beds. These are equal opportunity annoyances, and even if they are harder to endure sitting up most of the night in coach, we wish our more comfortable companions well. There is no envy on a train.

- There are always slow freights, flash floods, or confused cows that show up at the most inconvenient times.

- Everybody has a story to share on a train. Community seating in the dining car is designed to encourage making new acquaintances, but you don't need a social director on the rails. We are social by nature.

- We travel to fulfill every conceivable human need. A woman and her teenage son return from visiting relatives in the East while the husband and father stays at home to care for his critically ill father. The day after we meet in the dining car, I see bad news reflected in the woman's face, and she tells me the old man has died. A young man from the South joins his aging father in Ohio to share an adventure that will eventually take them above the Arctic Circle and strengthen the deep affection and respect they obviously have for one another. An American original boards the train at an isolated spot on the Great Plains. He lives in a town of nine hundred people, six hundred miles from the nearest hospital and is traveling to the coast for a family wedding. We talk for a long time before we get around to asking each other what we do. A train conversation always starts with "Where are you going?" never with "What do you do?" When he eventually asks and I tell him I am a psychologist, he replies that he is a welder who once had dinner with Karl Menninger.

- This world through which we travel is full of beauty, both the natural beauty of lakes, rivers, plains, mountains, and seas, and the man-made beauty of towering cities and simple prairie towns. Sadly, we are often too busy to notice.

- We pass through long stretches of empty landscapes, and our eyes are locked on the unrelieved desolation. If we turn away from the window, we might miss the fort where Sitting Bull surrendered or fail to notice how green fades almost imperceptibly to brown as we enter the high desert. Desolation has its own kind of beauty.

- Where there is no rain, there is no rust. The man sitting next to me stares intently out the window when we pass vehicles abandoned on the plains, and he spots the frame of a one-hundred-year-old Model A Ford. He tells me he is keeping track of these locations with plans to recover and restore another car for his collection. Just when we think we have heard about everything that can capture the passion of the human spirit, this fellow shows up with his scavenger's eye, mechanic's hands, and collector's zeal. There is no limit to human interests or resourcefulness.

- When we emerge from the thick evergreen forests of central Washington, the sea is with us again, oddly to our right when we turn south. We are on the West Coast, a mirror image of our Eastern home, but only from our egocentric, limited point of view. Everywhere is home for somebody.

So here we are, our trip ended, our experiment complete. Does the metaphor of life as a train journey have anything to teach us, and if so, do we learn it better if we actually live the metaphor? The answer is obvious, but I wonder if the lessons endure or if they need to be repeated.

Since my return, I have not been on another train or, for that matter, any public conveyance that simulates the experience. Unless something changes soon, I am limited to whatever insight I can glean from riding the hospital elevator. But that's okay. With all of its ups and downs, it has its possibilities.

Adapted from *New England Psychologist*, October 2010.

• • •

FINDING A NEW WAY TO LISTEN

It's the kind of conversation that might occur anywhere two reasonably sociable strangers find themselves sharing time together waiting for something to happen—a long line at the registry of motor vehicles, a tedious train or bus ride, an unforeseen delay in the airport's departure lounge.

It's the kind of conversation we usually try to avoid, burying our noses in the daily paper or a good book. Sometimes, however, we get hooked as I did one day not long ago. My partner in this dialogue began with a comment about our shared predicament in heavily accented English, and before I knew it, I was caught up in a story that would show me a new way to listen.

It was a story of growing up in a distant land familiar to me only through news dispatches from that part of the world so often beset by social revolution and natural disasters.

It was familiar too because my companion and I were of similar age, his boyhood and mine running along parallel lines of development oceans and continents apart. He spoke of events that had held the world's attention for a time and, like most international crises, faded into the background when more urgent developments took their place.

If these events affected me at all, they did so in the way a compelling film or book temporarily raises our consciousness to important issues or by making life inconvenient as when an oil crisis causes gas prices to rise. But inconvenience, intellectual stimulation, and moral outrage are nothing compared to the effects of these same events on my companion's life.

He was a good storyteller, Coleridge's Ancient Mariner to my wedding guest. Like the wedding guest, when he holds me with his "glittering eye," I "cannot choose but hear." What I hear is a chronicle of history sprinkled with titillating insider information that comes either from my companion's life experience or rich imagination. He refers to historical figures of the time, periodically checking my memory and comprehension, and proceeds only after assuring himself that I am still following. Like a camera adjusting its field of view, he varies his perspective, zooming out for a wide-angle analysis of geopolitical forces and back in again to describe his small and quite accidental role in what became a grand historical drama.

He says little of his move to the United States and what happened since, but brief allusions to hard times and intrusive emotions tell me that he is a complicated and uneasy nexus of global and personal developments.

The train pulls into the station, the airplane starts to board, the registry clerk calls my number. Our time together comes to a close and we say goodbye, but thoughts of the encounter linger. For some reason, I think about how our interaction might have been different if it had taken place under different circumstances.

Had this man sought my professional services as a psychologist, I would have steered the conversation toward those glimpses of distress that he provided when describing the aftermath of his involvement in world affairs. I hope I would have also had the presence of mind to recognize the skill, courage, and resilience he showed throughout his life's adventures.

Alternatively, our encounter might have occurred in the classroom with me taking notes while the learned professor held forth on matters of international import. This talk would be no dry history lesson, no mechanical recitation of facts, but a thorough discussion and analysis of events, cast in the sparkling light of the teacher's lived experience.

We might have met in my mechanic's garage where the guys talk about the old country and what they were doing on the ground while I was getting the news from the media. My companion would have fit right in, trading his own stories of daily life under the old regime with theirs, nodding solemnly in agreement or voicing sharp opposition to opinions about the quality of life under different governments.

As it was, we did not meet in any of these places but in a chance encounter where I found myself listening in all three ways, as a psychologist, a student, and one of the guys in the garage.

As a result, I believe I learned more and understood my companion better than I would have with any single mode of listening. So why not listen the same way in the consulting room? When the ancient mariner shows up on our doorstep and blames his misfortunes on the albatross, we are in our therapeutic comfort zone and know exactly what to so. Let him appear with tales of shoddy construction of the merchant fleet or ships becalmed by global climate change, and our course of action is suddenly not so clear.

I don't know how long the effect will last, but at least for now, I watch the nightly news not as an epic movie but as a collection of biographies of millions of people I will never meet, until one of them starts telling his story.

From *New England Psychologist*, April 2011.

THE LADY IN THE CHAIR

It was time for her annual review, and she had been transferred only recently to my unit. A year in the hospital and this was the first time we would be talking together. The nurse pointed me in the direction of a woman sitting in the TV room in her bathrobe and slippers. We were strangers to each other, and I can only imagine how odd it must have seemed to her when I explained that I would like to speak with her about her past year in the hospital. To my delight, the woman smiled and followed my lead to a nearby consulting room.

The room was an unremarkable space with a nice view of the distant hills. It contained a table, one comfortable chair, and a hassock. Before I could even say I was going to get another chair, she was sitting on the hassock and motioning me to the chair.

The chair, she said, is for those in authority and assured me that she was fine just where she was. Nonsense, I protested, there are plenty of chairs around here, and there's no reason we shouldn't both be comfortable.

I proceeded to drag a hard-back chair from the next room for myself and invited her to use the easy chair already in place. If I sit there, she smiled, I will feel like a queen. She urged me to take the soft chair and cautioned me not to use the hassock where she warned me I would feel like a bum.

How sad, I thought, that this woman was drawn to a lowly place where she felt perfectly at home. She clearly recognized the benefits of rank and authority and perhaps even longed to experience them, but the queen's chair, the throne, was never intended for the likes of her.

Seconds passed or maybe only an instant. How do you measure time when it is crammed with feelings and dimly apprehended associations, flashes of incomplete thoughts and memories, all moving too quickly to seize and examine? This is the work of intuition, the answer that comes before you are aware that you have worked out the problem. There would be time later to reflect. In the moment, you can only act. And so we agreed to share the throne, ten minutes at a time, but she would have to go first while I started with the hard chair. We had no need of the lowly hassock.

In the days that followed, I set out to learn more about chairs. How did they come to be used, and why are they such readily accessible symbols of authority? From the web site *Random History*, I learned that chairs have been around since the Stone Age. Even before the first person fashioned a seat with a back and then sat down on it, relics of sculptures at Neolithic building sites pointed to the existence of chair and bench-like areas. While simple seats have been found in Chinese tombs dating between 20,000 and 40,000 BCE, records suggest that the vast majority of the Chinese did not use chairs, preferring instead to kneel on the ground and support their weight on their heels.

In the Western world, hieroglyphic evidence suggests that the Egyptians used chairs in all strata of society at least since the third millennium BCE, but the seat of honor was reserved for the Pharaoh. The ornate throne sealed in the tomb of King Tutankhamen in 1352 BCE bears witness to the exalted status of royalty.

Evidence of the early use of chairs and the progressive refinement of chair design has been found in Mesopotamia, Greece, and Rome through the time of the Visigoth invasion in 410 CE. From that time until the dawn of the Renaissance one thousand years later, the historical record is strangely silent on the subject of chairs.

What we do know suggests that chairs were scarce, and where they were used at all, they were reserved for the masters of the household, even in the wealthiest of families. With the emergence of a wealthy class of noblemen in the fifteenth century, the chair made a remarkable comeback. By the seventeenth century, the ornate thrones of monarchs like Louis IV, Queen Christina of Sweden, and Alexis I of Russia proclaimed the divine authority of royalty.

I knew none of this when we agreed to share the room's only armchair. It was enough that our shared culture and language gave us the pope's chair of Peter, seats of power, chairmen of the board, royal thrones, and chairs of learning at universities throughout the world.

On a personal level, there were the straight-backed chairs of my straight-backed youth, the wicker rocking chair we bought because it looked good and seemed comfortable, and the worn armchair favored by my wife's parents and our daughter's visiting cat. The woman's associations to chairs remained, like so much else about her, shrouded in mystery.

We went about the business of the interview. Why are you here? Do you have great faith in the future? Tell me as many words as you can in one minute that begin with the letter f.

Time passed, and the ten-minute mark for switching chairs came and went. After thirty minutes, the woman said it was time to exchange seats, and so we did, each of us, I hope, a little wiser, a little less like strangers.

From *New England Psychologist*, January 2015.

EXTRA PEOPLE

Flannery O'Connor has a powerful short story entitled "The Displaced Person" where she describes the impact of the arrival of a refugee family on a small Southern farm. The story is set in the period following World War II when masses of people left Central and Eastern Europe in the wake of Soviet occupation of their homelands.

In O'Connor's story, a local priest arranges the placement of one of these families on a farm owned by a widow and worked by black and white farmhands. The established laborers do not take kindly to the arrival of the foreigners with strange names and industrious work habits. The resulting conflict sets the story in motion toward the kind of dramatic climax for which O'Connor is well known.

I have suggested this story for a reading group of psychology staff and students because of its relevance for our work as psychologists and for the lives we try to lead as decent human beings.

Who are the strangers among us, and how do we treat them? Reading "The Displaced Person" reminded me of a boy in my first grade class. When I asked the adults around me about his strange-sounding name, they said only that he was a DP, giving me the impression that he was of a class of people somehow inferior to the rest of us and not welcome in our town.

My onetime classmate left the stage of my memory long ago, but I have never forgotten his name or the derision he provoked in good people who should have known better. This experience was my introduction to the kind of bigotry and clannishness that flared up whenever new immigrant groups settled in our small corner of the world.

There was nothing unique about that time and place. It could have happened in any town in any country of the world. Each succeeding wave of immigrants threatened the order established by earlier waves.

DPs moved into the territory of naturalized Poles, Ukrainians, and Czechs. Puerto Ricans followed the DPs, and after them, came the Asians. Here in New England, where I have lived for nearly a half-century, it was the Irish and Italians who moved into the precincts of the Boston Brahmins, and everywhere the newcomers were the extra people.

We are never at a loss for extra people. They are the ones whom we now describe as marginalized, a word that was not in use when O'Connor wrote "The Displaced Person" in the early 1950s.

The extras are the racial and ethnic minorities among us, the mentally and physically challenged, psychiatric patients, prisoners, the poor, the old, anyone at all who differs from the perceived norm of the population. With a candor that leaves no doubt about the inclusion of the jobless in this category, the British describe losing one's job as being made redundant. One day you are a vital part of the workforce, and the next, you are redundant, no longer needed, in a word, extra.

The easiest way to fall into the extra category in our society is simply to grow old, especially when aging robs us of the faculties that allow us to function independently. In the past several months, I have been spending a lot of time in assisted living facilities, memory care centers, rehab units, and nursing homes.

My wife and I made the rounds as we settled a family member into a new residence with a higher level of support after a broken leg in her ninety-ninth year accelerated her declining ability to care for herself. Nearly all of the places where our loved one stayed to regain her strength were filled to capacity with people at widely different levels of cognitive and physical ability.

There was the man with Alzheimer's disease who sat in his wheelchair the whole day long speaking gibberish. Whenever we visited, his son was there engaging him in a companionable interchange, using words and gestures that the old man seemed to understand at least on the most important level of knowing that someone cared.

A woman sat with her head bowed and summoned me with a flutter of her hand. In a barely audible voice, she said we had to get out of this place and asked if I could bring her to her room. Another woman was mentally sharp and sociable, and as she told us her life story, we were surprised to learn how much we had in common. She came from the same town as my wife, went to the same school twenty years earlier, and raised her family not far from where we raised ours. We discovered that we went to the same church and knew many of the same people.

Later, in another facility, our introductions to the residents came with asides about what they had accomplished before dementia ushered them into the company of the displaced.

O'Connor's story ends with the insight that there are no displaced persons. Because her characters are here in the setting where she put them, they have a place. As with all great literature, we see ourselves in O'Connor's displaced persons. They are here and so are we, each and every one of us so close to being extra that the word loses its meaning.

Adapted from *New England Psychologist*, May 2015.

TWO

LOSS, CHANGE, AND SADNESS

There is no place like a mental hospital to get a close up look at loss, change, and sadness—no place on earth, except in our own hearts. The whole process of growth and maturation entails an accumulation of losses. With every step forward, we move away from a source of security—mother, family, school—toward an unknown and uncertain future. Under the best of circumstances, the future brings a certain amount of what the world calls success, prosperity, and contentment, but there is always a price to pay. People come and go in our lives, and every commitment we make to one course of action brings with it the sad task of renouncing all other possibilities.

For those who suffer from serious and persistent mental illness, losses multiply faster than the ability to let go of shattered dreams of a normal life. The stories in this chapter address the challenge of letting ourselves experience our sadness so that we can find new dreams when the old ones fail.

While the theme of loss threads its way throughout this collection, I have grouped these four essays, written between 1995 and 1999, into one chapter perhaps representing my attempt to confront the issue directly at a time when I was becoming more aware of my own sadness.

By 1995, I had experienced the loss of my first career path as an outpatient child psychologist when the Commonwealth of Massachusetts privatized outpatient clinics in 1990. After a year working on an adult inpatient unit at the Solomon Carter Fuller Mental Health Center in Boston, I learned that the Commonwealth was starting to contract with private agencies to provide all psychological services within the city of Boston.

I was fortunate to have the option to transfer to the Gaebler Children's Center in suburban Waltham, Massachusetts, but the Department of Mental Health closed that storied institution six months after my arrival.

In October of 1992, I presented myself on the doorstep of the psychology department at Westborough State Hospital, where over the next eighteen years, I built a career working with people with serious mental illness, helping to develop and then co-directing an APA-accredited psychology internship, and supervising students.

My time at Westborough State Hospital was, by and large, happy and productive though, when I wrote these columns, I was still adjusting to the changes and learning the dimensions of the new challenges and opportunities that I was encountering every day.

Family life, as always, was a refuge from the stress of the hospital but not without its own challenges. My father died in May of 1996 in a New Jersey hospital, two weeks after we saw him during a road trip to visit prospective colleges for our daughter who was finishing her junior year in high school.

As an only child living at a distance from my parents, I had helped my mother with his care as best I could over the preceding ten years, consulting with his doctors in New Jersey, seeking information from my colleagues in Boston, and once arranging a consultation with a very helpful neurologist at the Boston University Medical Center with which I was affiliated at the time. My father's loss surely made me more aware of my own sadness and that of the patients I wrote about in these columns.

In the stories that follow, you will find references to my wife and son and, in later chapters, to my daughter. I will not try to describe them here out of respect for their privacy and recognition of my inability to capture the wonderful complexity of who they are. I hope that the glimpses of them provided in this book will accumulate into a picture that will show how individually and collectively, they are the foundation of all that I do.

As a psychologist, I cannot talk about loss, change, and sadness without also talking about ways to manage the mental suffering that these experiences provoke. Ever since I first saw the rings of Saturn through a telescope when I was eleven, one of my favorite diversions and ways of managing distress has been astronomy. I entered college with the intention of studying to be an astronomer, and though I pursued psychology instead, the beauty of the night sky and the perspective it affords have never lost their appeal.

During my tenure at Westborough State Hospital, I started an astronomy group, brought in a telescope for observing sessions with patients, and published an essay about what we learned in the astronomy magazine *Sky and Telescope*. When a reader in England wrote to us about how astronomy helped him to overcome his depression, we recognized a kindred spirit, another strand in the bond of our common humanity, and the world grew that much smaller.

We begin this section with the essay "A Piece of the Universe" and the effort to gather light from darkness.

A PIECE OF THE UNIVERSE

With his round face and silver hair radiant in the bright morning sunlight, my visitor announced that he felt like a comet. He made this startling assertion after we had walked down the long hill from the locked part of the hospital to my office in the open building where he once lived. The building was scheduled to be closed as a residence hall, and it seemed to me that my patient had come to say goodbye. He was saying goodbye even as he protested that he could magically reverse the course of events already bearing down on us like the cold fire of a million distant stars.

The comet reference was, in psychodynamic parlance, multi-determined, but the office itself set the stage for this kind of talk. The room's spare décor includes a large framed photograph of the planet Saturn and its moons taken from the Voyager II spacecraft. On the bulletin board above the desk is a small cartoon depicting an observatory bearing a cautionary sign, "Warning. Astronomy may be hazardous to your sense of self-importance."

How odd, I sometimes think, that I have chosen to display such a message in a house of self-improvement, but maybe it's just the perspective that we need. The bookshelf on the opposite wall contains a stack of astronomy magazines and a binder full of my own photographs of the night sky.

It is to this binder that my patient turns his attention, asking me once again to identify the Northern Cross, the North American Nebula, the Andromeda galaxy, and the Southern Milky Way.

He speaks the words over and over as if trying to gain his bearings, to fix his own position in space and time, building boundaries of sound and science around his manic flight of ideas. He is reminded of ancient camping trips when he gazed at the stars with his uncle, a man whose steady light still guides his course through the tedious routine of life as a mental patient.

That was so long ago, and so much has changed: mental illness, loves lost and others never found, remaining stuck in time while friends and family move on to meet new challenges and opportunities.

"Nebulas. I don't like nebulas," the patient announces. Does he know, I wonder, that these ghostly puffs of gas are stars being born or dying? "A piece of the universe," he continues, "is missing." There is reason enough here to dislike nebulas when so much of his own personal universe has already been lost.

We are looking at a photograph of the North American Nebula, a vast expanse of interstellar gas and dust glowing with the energy of nearby stars, exciting hydrogen atoms into a quiet frenzy of soft red light. Dark matter obscures this light in just the right places to produce a shape resembling the continent of North America.

Astronomers estimate the distance of the North American Nebula to be somewhere between three hundred and three thousand light years away. In any case, we are looking at a photograph of the way this region of the night sky appeared long before either of us was born. We are looking into the past into a great celestial furnace where new stars are being forged. For all we know, they may already be there.

What lights give their energy to this visitor in my office? He is a talented musician who can rise above his fears, impulses, and disorganized thought patterns in flights of sweet, coherent melody. What stars of achievement of even modest steps toward independent living are being born in the cauldron of his tortured passions? The North American Nebula is a birthplace of stars, but other nebulas are the remnants of violent explosions or the sloughed off shells of quietly fading lights. There is no gain without the risk of loss.

My patient does not like nebulas, but he feels like a comet. "How so?" I ask, thinking of a comet's lonely journey from the farthest reaches of the solar system to its glorious burst of light as it nears the sun. "Beautiful like a comet," he replies.

I have never seen the North American Nebula, though I have captured it on film. This phenomenon is familiar to astronomers who know that the light of faint celestial objects can be collected like raindrops in a barrel. When the barrel is full, the image floats to the surface.

Astronomers also know that it is sometimes best not to look for an object exactly where it is known to be. More efficient is the strategy of averted vision, glimpsing a faint source of light, like a distant comet, from the more sensitive corners of our eyes. Astronomers know a thing or two about how to gather light, and so do psychologists. We call it insight. We will listen patiently as long as we must to collect its fragments and delight in finding it hovering around the edges of our attention.

From *Massachusetts Psychologist*, April 1995.

●●●

A SLOW, SILENT FIRE

Be careful what you wish for, the adage goes, because your wish might come true. Last April, after another bleak and gray New England winter, I found myself wishing, as I always do every spring, for those first green leaves to cover the world again.

But times change, and green hope runs its course, exploding in the glory of mature red and gold, falling back to earth in windblown brown. So now I stand raking, knee-deep in the remains of springtime wishes, exhilarated for a while by the bright sun, crisp air, and the feeling of muscles asleep too long in the therapist's chair.

This week, the therapist's chair once again has brought me George, or to be completely honest, I have brought the chair to him. I find myself doing this a lot at the hospital, pursuing patients grateful afterwards for having had the opportunity to talk but too disorganized, ambivalent, or uncomfortable to keep appointments on their own initiative.

George is a tall, muscular man in his mid-forties whose broad, swarthy face is contorted in a perpetual scowl. He has been episodically violent toward others but more often abusive to himself. From his early teens, he has turned to drugs and alcohol, petty larceny, and gambling for the excitement he hopes will wipe away the feelings of sadness and despair that have made their uneasy home in a heart broken by repeated and overwhelming loss.

I am thinking of George as I rake, and I find my exhilaration giving way to fatigue as I am overwhelmed by more leaves than I can handle. Not only do they fall from the sky but also seem to be crawling up out of the cracked and broken earth. Even so, the raking is not as bad as the job of leveling and disposing of the enormous mounds that turn the yard into a Himalayan range of leaves.

In this, my seventeenth year of tending this patch of earth, you'd think I would have discovered the most efficient strategy for dealing with the problem, that I would know exactly what to do. The truth is I have discovered several perfect solutions, each one lasting a few years and then bowing before a different, if not necessarily better, idea.

When I was younger, more energetic, and naively enamored of a neat and pristine landscape, my wife and I actually bagged every leaf in the yard. We struggled to keep the bags open until we had dropped just enough leaves into each bag for it to stand on its own, mouth agape, waiting for more.

The experience taught me to describe my real estate not only by the features and area of its terrain, but also by its annual yield of leaves: one hundred bags, more or less—one hundred bags, neatly tied, packed in every square inch of the car only five times, if we were lucky, and quietly put out of the way in the town dump. The procedure was exhausting, but the results were neat, clean, almost surgically pure.

This week, George got his first paycheck from his new job at the local supermarket. The money lasted exactly one day, hardly more time than it took him to spend every last dime on lottery scratch tickets. When he realized he had nothing left, he sold his stash of coffee at black market prices to some of his fellow patients. Immediately, he put his profits into more scratch tickets.

"When I walk around with those tickets in my pocket," George told me, "I feel terrific, and I know I could feel that way forever if I never checked to see if I had a winner." Just before his spending spree, George learned that the aunt who had cared for him after the deaths of his mother and grandparents had just had a serious heart attack.

It is too hard to collect one hundred bags of leaves every year, and so we began to haul them up the long hill on tarpaulins to the front of the house where a man we hired gathered them into his truck and carried them away.

"I can't talk any more Doctor. Can we stop now? I don't feel good. I have a headache and I need to lie down." It's the sadness, George. Can't you see? No amount of gambling or stealing or drugs or sleeping will take it away. Let me help you learn to bear your sorrow so you can heal. Poets and great theorists of psychotherapy have told us that sadness, if borne patiently, can transform our lives. They might as well have been speaking to George.

This year, I will not cart the fallen leaves away but pile them discretely in a corner of the yard at the bottom of the hill. There nature's slow, silent fire will turn them to rich black soil to replenish the bare spots in a landscape too pure for its own good.

Adapted from *Massachusetts Psychologist*, December 1995.

• • •

THE RELUCTANT
KING OF THE MOUNTAIN

Nearly a year has passed since I pronounced the perfect solution to raking up and disposing of New England's legendary foliage that annually carpets the piece of earth I call my own. In the compost heap, nature's alchemy magically turns dull, brittle leaves into the black gold of life-giving soil.

The process is not unlike the transformation that occurs in the human heart when our losses and sadness are given a place of their own—a center of influence from which waves of change can turn us into new people better prepared to meet life's challenges.

Nearly a year has passed too since I put my words into action and made the compost pile that I described so enthusiastically. When our work in the yard was done, my wife topped off the day with a surprise screening of the perfect movie for the occasion.

You and Your Compost Pile by the U.S. Department of Agriculture may have lacked the star quality, drama, adventure, and romance of some of its competitors, but it certainly made up for those minor deficiencies by packing a wallop of useful information.

In less time than it took to finish the popcorn, I learned all that I needed to know about compost piles. But I still had trouble believing that this mountain of leaves in my yard would ever disappear and become the very earth from which they originally grew.

And so I began to ask friends and neighbors about their experiences with such matters. Do you have a compost pile? What do you put in it? One fellow told me that he added bacteria, actually packaged and sold for the express purpose of helping along the composting process.

But the question behind the question, as psychotherapists are fond of saying, was always, "How long does it take?" The nagging anxiety in my heart, the dread that only now can be admitted, was simply this: "What if it doesn't work? What if the pile of leaves is still there, big as ever next fall when a new onslaught of foliage lays claim to the yard?"

In its raw, most terrifying form, the question was really, "What happens if we are buried by leaves?"

The deep winter snows did their part in hiding the compost pile and quelling my anxiety. When spring began to uncover the yard, the heap of leaves seemed smaller. Were they just matted down, or had they begun to decompose?

Soon I developed the habit of adding my grass clippings to the mix and actually began to enjoy this new ending of the weekly lawn mowing ritual. I was the high priest presiding over the mire with pitchfork in hand, the reluctant King of the Mountain, standing not at the summit but warily at the base to avoid the slithering mass of worms and thousand-leggers prodded into action with each turn of the fork.

In time, this mess of life began to spawn a feeling of satisfaction, a sense of closure and complicity in the flow of time and the changes it brings.

When I stand before this altar of sludge, I think of my patients—often of a man addicted to drugs and gambling who ran from the sadness of his life the way I ran to the town dump with dead leaves I preferred to forget. A year has come and gone, and my patient is still running from his past, but he has begun to hobble, if not to run, toward his future.

Before this pile of compost, I sometimes think of myself and the losses this year has brought. Sometimes my reverie is broken by the thud of the pitchfork striking a twig or rock embedded in the decaying leaves. Not all of this will turn to soil, but I am finally beginning to believe that most of it will. Though I am still a bit skeptical, after a year I am as surprised by those unexpected lumps in the pile as I am by those uninvited lumps in the throat that come with the autumn wind.

The other day, I uncovered a small, blue plastic man who had the misfortune to fall into the mire. I could not make a positive identification, but I knew at once that he was not one of the fabled superheroes my son stations around our house and yard.

Iron Man, Wolverine, Olympus . . . any of those guys would have made it look simple to emerge unscathed from this mess that life can throw our way. "He's just some guy," my son said, unimpressed. "Nobody special."

"Of course, silly me," I shrugged, even as a smile of hope started to break across my face.

From *Massachusetts Psychologist*, November 1996.

Before the Fall

It is quiet on the hospital grounds, so quiet that on blustery spring days, the loudest sound is the wind. Two lakes and acres of farmland seal us off from the noise of traffic on Route 9 less than a mile away. Although there is an airport within twenty miles, we are not located on a flight path, and it is rare to hear the sound of an airplane. When one passes, it is high overhead, glints of silver moving soundlessly across the sky.

My companion and I stand in silence while he smokes two cigarettes down to the filter. He almost burns the tips of his fingers because he will not let go until he has drained the life out of each slender stalk. We hear the throbbing of a helicopter's rotors long before it comes into view. The sound builds, and we lift our eyes to this determined intruder slashing the air high over our heads.

"I have never flown in a helicopter," my companion says. I think his comment is peculiar because of all the other more ordinary things I know he has never done. He has never lived in a place of his own, never driven a car to work and back, never cooked a dinner for his friends, never married, never had children.

For this man, schizophrenia lived up to its earlier name, *dementia praecox* or "youthful insanity," and cut short his own youth. From the onset of his illness in his early twenties, my companion has been at a disadvantage. He has lived with all of the needs, desires, ambitions, and challenges of his healthy peers but without the capacity to respond effectively.

I am not surprised that he has never flown in a helicopter, but I am surprised that of all the things he has missed in life, this one seems to matter. When I remark that I know he has flown in an airplane when he traveled abroad after graduating from high school, he adds that he also once took flying lessons.

The man goes on in his halting manner of speech to explain how he had taken a few introductory flying lessons at a small airfield near his college before he got sick. Now I am surprised, and I try to imagine the man twenty years younger, clean shaven, looking like the college student he once was, bending his tall, slender frame into the cockpit of a small airplane to take his place beside a crisp flight instructor. Soon they are airborne, and the instructor hands over the controls to my companion, and for a brief time, he soars.

To think of my companion flying an airplane is to see what he might have been and to be stunned by the distance he has fallen from the goals he once thought himself able to achieve. If indeed he had begun to take flying lessons, then he once had the courage and sense of adventure to begin transforming the universal dream of flight into a personal reality.

When he tells me he once took flying lessons, I think but do not say, "You did it, you actually did it, but I only dreamed it." It was enough for me, as a boy, to imagine a bunch of helium filled balloons on each of my bedposts and to see myself flying over the house, the yard, the factories, and the marshland.

Once, I invented a flying machine consisting of two giant magnets mounted above a metal floor. The scientific principle was something like trying to make yourself jump by pulling on your shoelaces. It doesn't work. Still, my friend Bobby and I pretended to be jet fighter pilots and raided the neighbor's woodpile for scraps to build an airplane big enough to sit in, but too heavy to move.

The sound of the helicopter gradually fades as it shuttles out of sight, and my companion and I are once again alone in silence. I have known this man for years, but today he has told me something that makes me see him in a new light. My instinct is to believe him, or is it just my wish? How many times have I heard claims of elevated status, unimaginable wealth, of fantastic achievements from people made powerless by mental illness? Perhaps my companion's claim of flight is just another grandiose delusion, born in a shattered mind looking for a sense of accomplishment.

But then why stop at telling me about a few flying lessons? To reveal something he has never accomplished, something he has tried but given up hardly seems grandiose. He could have told me he once was a jet fighter pilot, or that he flew commercial airplanes, or simply that he had done what he had set out to do—and learned to fly.

The historical truth of my companion's statement may never be known. But there is truth here of a different kind. He wants me to know that he once had high aspirations but fell to the state in which I see him now.

Like my companion, I too had dreams of flight before I learned that there is more than one way to soar. So I stand here today as his psychologist, not his flight instructor, reminded of how much he wanted—and trying even now to help him—to do what he can.

Originally published as "Fear of Flying Need Not Get in the Way" in *Massachusetts Psychologist*, May 1999.

THREE

ONE PERFECT LIFE

The ancient Greeks have given us the radical idea that each of our lives, no matter how long or short, is perfect simply because it is uniquely ours. This notion is hard enough to accept even when our lives are lucky. When life is filled with illness, loss, and sadness, the challenge of seeing it as perfect can seem insurmountable.

In his discussion of human development, psychologist Erik Erikson described integrity as the final achievement and culmination of a life experienced as having turned out exactly as it should have. Like the Greek sages before him, Erikson did not mean that our lives ever unfold precisely as we wish. He is talking about an attitude that enables us to look back on our lives and see that we have done well enough with all of the challenges, disappointments, and opportunities that have come our way.

While integrity may be the end point or goal of life, its development begins in childhood with the recognition that we have been set down at this particular time in this particular place, and there isn't a thing we can do about it.

My particular time and place began in 1947 Carteret, New Jersey, Exit 12 on the turnpike, seen from that highway as a place of refineries, oil storage tanks, and the bright flame of industrial gases burning from the top of a steel tower. Yet in my memory, it is also a place of Independence Day parades, picnics in the park, basketball and tennis courts, and labyrinthine paths through acres of marsh grass taller than our heads.

There, a boy could lose himself in imaginary adventures, and that's just what my friends and I did. We called the place Youknow-where so I could give my mother a truthful but evasive answer to her question of where I had been when I came back from that forbidden playground. In winter, my parents pulled me up and down the long hill though the center of town on my Flexible Flyer sled—a happy memory but, sadly, one of the few I have of my parents pulling together on anything.

I grew up in a house without central heating or a telephone. There was no family car after my father's collision with a utility pole when I was five. As an only child, I had no one with whom to share the burden of our deprivations or the love that each of my parents managed to show me despite the strains and conflicts of their uneasy alliance.

My parents gave me the best education available in Catholic elementary and high schools, and I continued my education at Villanova University and then at Boston University, where I earned my doctorate in clinical psychology in 1975.

My life has been rich in friendship, the love of my wife and children, and opportunities to use my talents to serve others in work that I have found meaningful and rewarding. Despite my challenges, disappointments, losses, and failures, I cannot think of my life as anything but fortunate. While I would not claim to have achieved the Greek ideal of the perfect life or Erikson's goal of integrity, I can imagine getting there in time.

When I decided to become a psychologist, I did not plan to devote the major portion of my career to working with people challenged by severe mental illness. It happened, as I have come to believe all things happen, through a combination of choice and chance.

In the straightened circumstances and atmosphere of conflict that permeated my childhood, my family of origin was not typical, even for our time and place. Perhaps this is why I have often felt like an outsider, the kid looking through the window at others enjoying life the way it was supposed to be.

I remember the woman everyone called Crazy Molly, a loud, brash, disorganized woman who marched through the streets of our little town. It would be nice to say that I was curious about her and that this curiosity motivated me to become a psychologist. The truth is that I noticed her and made other plans for my day and my life. That I remember her today has more to do with where I wound up and how I learned along the way that, no matter how strange or different people look or behave, every one of us is trying to make a life that makes sense and has meaning.

This is the perfect life of the Greek sages, Erikson's crown of integrity, and what Erasmus, the fifteenth-century Dutch philosopher, called happiness, the wish to be who you are. The essays in this chapter tell the stories of people searching for this elusive prize and the special challenges of that quest for people with mental illness.

SOME THOUGHTS ON
INTEGRITY IN THE ASYLUM

These days, in my work with the chronically mentally ill, I find myself thinking a lot about integrity. I am not just talking about honor, although that is a part of it, but rather the idea of integrity described by Erik Erikson as the sense of being whole or complete that comes with a natural acceptance of one's life.

Recently, my thoughts on this subject were brought into sharp focus during a lunchtime walk through the museum documenting the history of Westborough State Hospital.

The two corridors of the museum led me through a bygone era of peculiar diagnoses, photographs of elegantly appointed buildings designed for a rest cure in the country, antique medical instruments, and pictures of patients and staff frozen forever in time.

The faces of the staff openly meet the curious eyes of visitors, but the gazes of the patients are blocked by black rectangles put there to disguise their identities. With the exception of that one distinguishing feature, patients and staff are alike in their handsome Victorian dress and in the intensity of their studied poses.

In one such pose, a gray-haired man leans over a table where other men and women wearing black rectangles are absorbed in what looks like an art project. Was it his sympathetic ear, his firm but kindly guidance that contributed to their recovery? Or was it the chance to rest, the clean country air, the healing waters of the hydrotherapy spa, or merely the passage of time that brought recovery to the patients of this hospital one hundred years ago?

The proudly displayed statistics show that some patients indeed recovered from mental illnesses thought to have been caused by apoplexy, business trouble, dissipation, domestic trouble, intemperance, habitual drunkenness, and, yes, even overwork.

The simplicity of these early ideas about the causes and cures of mental illness brings a smile to my face. Then I remember the recent past of my own early days of training in psychology and the interesting hypotheses about possible biological bases for schizophrenia and depression competing with other theories implicating faulty early relationships, loss, and disturbed patterns of communication in families. Now we speak of biopsychosocial models of etiology with many arguing for an accent on the first syllable, but with time, even this mindset may change.

Change. In the end, everything changes except for the presence of patients, staff, and a script that brings us together in a drama as old as the history of suffering and compassion. I wander through the museum like an actor looking at the pictures of my predecessors who graced the stage on opening nights in the distant past. I feel a kinship with the man leaning over the table who represents my own professional roots. As in any long-running production, the play outlasts the actors, and casts come and go.

Suddenly I am distracted by the loud voice of a patient looking at the exhibits. The man has been in the hospital a long time and will probably always require some form of institutional care. He laughs nervously as he reads aloud to his companion the word "insane" in the hospital's first official title. The word falls harshly on our modern sensibilities, and I think I see the patient wince.

As the man proceeds through the museum, I wonder if he feels a connection to the patients in the photographs. Does he recognize his own role in this smash hit of a tragedy, breaking records for the longest runs on the Broadways of hospital grounds everywhere? And, if he does, can he integrate that role with his life and still preserve a sense of wholeness, honor, integrity, or at least, self-acceptance?

This task is not easy in a society where everyday attitudes about the mentally ill lag far behind our more enlightened understanding of their illnesses. I think of the wounded honor of another patient who told me how, on a recent shopping trip, a woman cautioned her young son to stay away from the "bad man."

What is the purpose of a life shattered by mental illness? How can we find meaning in our wounds, dignity in roles that we did not choose to play, and a new direction when the road we travel crumbles beneath our feet? To join our patients in their search for answers to these questions is the ultimate honor and challenge of our work with the mentally ill.

Adapted from *Massachusetts Psychologist*, December 1993.

• • •

THIS PINEWOOD LIFE

An old joke asks, how do you carve an elephant? You start with a block of marble and chip away everything that doesn't look like an elephant.

Today I am thinking not of marble but of wood—a rectangular piece of pine, exactly seven inches long, one and three-quarter inches high.

I have no interest in carving elephants, but I am determined to help my eight-year-old son turn this humble piece of wood into a racing car. As Cub Scouts and their parents have done for years, we are entering the annual Pinewood Derby where we will display and race the car that is left over after we have chipped away everything else.

To build a Pinewood car, it is helpful to have four basic instructions or at least a list of tips that others have found useful.

First, open the package and inspect its contents. You will find one block of pine, four plastic wheels, and four nails. Everyone starts with the same basic materials, but it is your own ingenuity, skill, and experience that will fashion a car that is like no other.

A life, like a Pinewood car, begins with basic materials and is shaped by the interplay of chance and choice.

A recent *Time* magazine article asks how nature carves a brain. You begin with an embryo, standard issue, yet almost every one is genetically different. You start with all the nerve cells you will ever have and, over the next ten years or so, add generous helpings of sensory experience. Through this process, you build trillions more connections between neurons than your brain will ever need.

Then, as the little-used connections wither and die of neglect, you will have chipped away everything that doesn't look like the particular brain that is yours alone and unlike any other.

Secondly, you should take some time to decide on the basic shape of your car. Templates are available in many hobby shops, or you can draw the outline of your own design on the wooden block.

At Pinewood Derby time, the older boys—who have traded in their Cub Scout gear for the trappings of adolescence—are always willing to lend a hand. At church on Sunday, my son finds a teenage friend and former Pinewood winner. He tells us the secret is in a sleek, aerodynamic design and in well-balanced wheels and lubricated axels. Our daughter's boyfriend simply sends over two of the cars he made in his own Cub Scout days, so we can see for ourselves what works best. In the hospital, a colleague shares the secrets of her son's winning car.

We shape our lives by the example of others. In my own times of crisis, I am grateful to my older friends and colleagues who share their own experiences on the rough path that I may be just beginning to travel.

Recently, a friend just starting out in our profession asked me how to build a career in psychology. At this Pinewood time of the year, I was tempted to tell him you start with a life and chip away everything that doesn't look like a career in psychology.

But then what is left of the life? The question has no easy answer, and he is too perceptive to believe such advice from a man wearing a Pocahontas bandage where the chisel slipped in Pinewood days.

Thirdly, secure the pine block with a clamp or in a vise and cut away the excess wood.

The cutting is decisive. Your decision to cut one shape and not another may later seem unwise. Some irregularity in the wood grain or clumsiness in your technique may produce a shape you never intended to make. Either way, you learn to live with the result.

At eight, my son is just realizing the richness and complexity of the grain of his life. At nearly fifty, I am still making unwise and clumsy cuts and wishing I could take them back.

Next, mount the wheels, add weights, and paint your car in a color scheme of your choice.

Now we sit around the kitchen table, the family brought together by this Pinewood project. With her loving attention to detail and generous spirit, my wife helps to prepare four smooth, shiny nails, the axels around which the hopes of a small boy will spin down a wooden track. She gives our son her artist's brushes for the final step.

Our son likes the painting and decorating best, and he produces a shiny green car with yellow and silver trim. We all hope it will do well on race day, but it has already served a more important purpose.

With its rough surfaces and uneven cuts, it is not exactly the car our boy had in mind.

But it is his car, and that is reason enough for him to love it.

From *Massachusetts Psychologist*, March 1997.

• • •

DISCOVERING THE
MESSAGE OF BENZONI'S RULER

The drugstore near the hospital where I visit with my patient is a long way from the London street market where I found Benzoni's ruler. The drugstore also carries rulers, the most notable of which is the All-Purpose Rolling Ruler. I have taken the time to study this remarkable instrument while my patient compulsively scans rows of medicated skin creams that offer the promise of self-sufficient health care in the world beyond the hospital walls.

I have even briefly considered buying an All-Purpose Rolling Ruler, intrigued by its six different features. These clear plastic gizmos function as a parallel ruler, compass, protractor, T-square, and, get this, a vertical ruler and a horizontal ruler. Yes, that's right, there are six, count 'em, six different functions. Of course, to get six functions, you have to accept the marketing premise that there is something special about a ruler that can be used in both vertical and horizontal positions.

They can't fool me. This is where I draw the line, or would, if I owned a decent ruler. But I know exaggeration when I see it, and so I leave the All-Purpose Rolling Ruler on the shelf.

Still, I find myself wanting to make some use of these observations with my patient, to acknowledge his concern about whether or not he will be able to keep himself safe and healthy after discharge, and to break into his stereotyped shelf scanning and label reading.

I think of the advertiser's emphasis on versatility, the idea of making the most of what you have, and I search for the few simple words that will help him recognize and develop his own special functions, the All-Purpose Rolling Man. But the language eludes me, my timing is off, and we are on to the next aisle.

Some things are better left unsaid.

A week later, I am in London with my family at the beginning of one of those vacations where you find yourself wondering what exactly it is you do back home. London is not so much a single city as it is a collection of villages and neighborhoods strung together by miles of Underground and arteries of bright red buses.

When you step off the deep, steep escalator in the tube station, there is no mistaking one stop for another. You are clearly in a different part of town. That day, we stepped out into a spring drizzle in the borough of Islington and wandered through narrow alleys of antique shops and bargain tables of weekend peddlers.

As in the drugstore near the hospital, a ruler once again attracted my attention. This ruler was in the window of a shop so small, I could barely squeeze down its single aisle without risking bric-a-brac carnage.

Averting destruction until the last minute, I made my way to a stand holding two twelve-inch wooden rulers. Reaching into the display, I grasped one but knocked over a few small items.

"No, no," fussed the owner, a bespectacled woman just the right size for the proportions of her miniature shop. I made my apology and, after some bargaining, my purchase.

My treasure is a twelve-inch ruler, fashioned from a lightweight, hard wood in mottled shades of brown. Ink-stained and smooth to the touch, it has the feel of age and use. "Pre-war," is all the woman could tell me, clarifying that she meant the first war.

On the back of the ruler, the name "C.M. Benzoni" is printed in the same black ink that randomly dots its surface. The front of the ruler bears in its center an imprint in small, block letters, "Adie & Son Edinburgh." Far to the left in letters almost too small to read are the words, "Engine Divided."

Both long margins of the ruler are marked off in thirtieths of an inch, with each third of an inch labeled from one through thirty-six. The edges of Benzoni's ruler are nicked and worn, no longer useful for drawing perfectly straight lines.

In spite of its many flaws, I did not hesitate to buy Benzoni's ruler. Except for an uncertain guess about its age, no one made any claims for its superiority, versatility, or usefulness. With Benzoni's ruler, what you see is what you get, and the way I see it, it provides something that the All-Purpose Rolling Ruler doesn't even approach. It has a history, a character, and a treasury of stories that I could never begin to guess.

While I will never know the content of his hopes and fears or the circumstances of his life, I know that C.M. Benzoni lived and dreamed and suffered and worked. When I pick up his ruler, I receive into my outstretched hand the baton of a teammate who ran the lap ahead of mine.

I turn instinctively to my drugstore companion, knowing there is a point to make about the value and nobility of each of our chipped and ink-stained lives. I turn even before the words come and I realize that he is an ocean away.

From *Massachusetts Psychologist*, June 1999.

BALANCING OUR THREE LIVES

We can envy the cat's nine lives or enjoy the three that are uniquely ours: the life we live, the life we tell, and the life we understand. Psychologists run the risk of overvaluing the examined life, assuming that every question put to us about human behavior calls for the most profound level of analysis of which we are capable.

You don't go to graduate school for four or more years, complete practicum, internship, and possibly postdoctoral training to provide anything less. Or do you?

The newcomer to the profession or to a new practice setting is especially vulnerable to the seductive charms of thorough analysis. This circumstance was recently made clear to me in an exit interview with one of our interns who looked back on his year of state hospital training astonished that he began with the assumption that a decision about whether a patient could safely take a pass to the mall required a full battery of psychological testing. Not that testing would not have been helpful, but we had equally useful information, and the patient had successfully managed similar passes. The clinical team simply needed a review of the patient's current mental status and recent behavior in order to make a decision about a very specific issue.

My empathy was immediate. When I started working here over a decade ago, I was not a newly minted psychologist, but new to an inpatient setting, I struggled over questions like which patients would be compatible roommates. Should Mr. Blaze, for example, with a childhood history of fire-setting motivated by poorly controlled anger at his father, the firefighter, be paired with Mr. Flush, the exuberant son of an obsessional plumber?

Some questions are easier than others, and this was a slam dunk, no-brainer. Of course, put the two of them together. On the remote chance that Mr. Blaze might try to defy authority by dropping a match, Mr. Flush would express his own defiance by filling pots and pans with water to douse the flames.

It turns out I was wrong. More than anything, Mr. Blaze needed his sleep, and Mr. Flush was a world-class snorer. No one said being a psychologist was going to be easy, but this seemed impossible.

The trick of course is to strike the proper balance between life lived and life understood. And let's not forget to add life told, since as therapists, we spend our days listening to others tell the stories of their lives.

A young man just beginning to understand what it means to have schizophrenia spends his time in therapy providing snapshots of his life before and after he first developed symptoms of his mental illness. There is little or no narrative continuity to these pictures that he spills as if from a broken photo album. Each one shows him at a very specific time and place.

He has the remarkable ability to recall exactly how he looked, what he was thinking, and how he behaved on specific dates over the past twenty years. He once came to the office with his pockets filled with slips of paper on each of which he had described a different moment in his life. One by one, he pulled out each slip, read it aloud, and told another fragment of his life story.

Over time, he has begun to place the pictures in his album in patterns that make sense. He speaks more about what he is doing every day and what he hopes to do in the future. Occasionally, he will still hold up individual snapshots for inspection, but he has learned that the blurred images belong to his illness and the clear ones, to the sustained periods of healthy functioning of which he is capable.

As the life he tells becomes the life he understands, he is free to enjoy the life that is there for him to live every day. And so are we all.

To live life as it is given to us is to live unselfconsciously and in the moment. Sages and scientists tell us that living this way requires a kind of wisdom that, sooner or later, comes to us all. No one said it better than a man whose thirty-year struggle with schizophrenia has taught him to make the most of each day. He chooses the present because "the future is filled with too many ifs, and the past, with too many if onlys."

The cat may have nine lives, but they are really only one life, repeated over and over again. We have only three but we live them simultaneously and, with luck, by artfully balancing living, telling, and understanding. The unexamined life may not be worth living, but the unlived life is no life at all.

From *New England Psychologist*, August/September 2005.

• • •

ON TIME, ONE MONTH LATE

It has always seemed to me that the most logical time to reflect on time is the beginning of the New Year in January. Of course, if I reflect on time at all, I usually do it in February. Here, I am tempted to offer a pseudo-philosophical explanation of this shortest month's unique relationship to psychological as well as calendar time.

Everyone knows that February is timeless—a short hiatus in the orderly march of events, a breathing space between the hectic pace of the holidays and the springtime promise of March. In other words, February is a deadly boring month with nothing much happening. So why not take this opportunity to reflect on the nature of time itself?

There is no time like the present and the present is the only time we have. The past is memory and the future, imagination. As clock time is defined, the only reality is now. If we were limited to clock time, this would be a problem because every "now" would become "then" as quickly as it happened.

Fortunately, our human nature comes with the capacity for both memory and imagination, and those uniquely human abilities enlarge our experience of time to include both past and future. We move flexibly between present, past, and future even when we are firmly established in the present. This fluidity is usually adaptive and is especially evident in our work as psychologists.

Recently, I participated in a special consultation regarding one of our long-term patients whose condition has steadily worsened throughout the many years she has been struggling with schizophrenia. A recent spate of medical problems and an increase in troublesome behavior had prompted a referral to a specialist in psychopharmacology who met with the clinical team before the patient and her elderly mother arrived.

In the traditional recitation of the patient's history, we told the consultant of the many hardships the patient and her family had faced in the thirty years she has been hospitalized. Only last year, the woman's brother committed suicide, and the family was still regaining its balance after this devastating loss. Then the patient's mother entered the room, old and frail, but with a look of determination in her eyes. She moved slowly, steadying herself on her heavy cane before each step. When the introductions had been made, the consultant turned toward the mother and expressed his condolences for the many tragedies he had just heard being enumerated in the family history.

The old woman cast a kindly eye in the direction of the consultant and then turned slowly, holding each of us for an instant in her wise and benevolent gaze. "Thank you for your concern," she said. "Yes, there have been tragedies, but it all happens gradually and that makes it manageable. And besides, there have been many good times as well."

At that moment, the family matriarch shone with integrity in her acceptance of all the hardships life had given her. Ten minutes before she entered the room, her only thought may have been the next step in her journey, quite literally, the now of each hobbled footstep from her car to the building and up two flights of stairs to the conference room. For those of us on the other side of the conference room door, however, our present was filled with the story of the family's past, presented (made present) as if it had unrolled before them in an instant.

Life happens gradually, one now after the other, until the whole story, beginning, middle, and end, is finally told. Thank goodness everything doesn't happen at once because, if it did, we could never cope with the intensity of our misfortune or the ecstasy of the graced moments that come to every life. The matriarch of our patient's family reminded us of this basic truth, so important in our lives and work that we teach it to our patients as a preferred coping strategy. Live in the moment. Survive the moment. Improve the moment. Let each moment, insignificantly small in itself, add to the imperceptibly accumulating aggregate of moments that makes each of our lives.

This is good advice to be sure, yet there is something more. Because of our uniquely human capacities for memory and imagination, within every present moment, we have the ability to revive the past and anticipate the future. We are time travelers without need of science fiction or modern technology to build time machines for our journey. Everything we need is in our heads, ready whenever we want to revisit the past for lessons learned or pleasures to savor, or to conjure up and prepare for the future. It doesn't matter whether we reflect on time in January or June, as long as we remain both captain and navigator of our incredible, self-contained time machines.

Adapted from *New England Psychologist*, February 2007.

• • •

BACK TO THE LIBRARY

One of the first excursions some of our patients take into the community is to the town library. For many, returning to the library restores a sense of normalcy lost when they became mentally ill and had to be hospitalized. The library offers a safe haven where everyone is welcome. Yet, when you fill out an application for a library card, you have to supply your address, and that can be awkward if you happen to be living in a state hospital. Not that anyone necessarily recognizes the hospital from its street address or that it would matter to them if they did. Still, you wonder.

It feels safer at the hospital, but you know that you have to take the next step if you hope to get on with your life. You'll go to the library next week, but now you have to hurry so you're not late for the Poetry and Fiction group. The group convenes every week in the front room of what was once the residence of the hospital's superintendents. It consists of men and women, white and black, in various stages of recovery from severe and persistent mental illnesses often complicated by histories of trauma and substance abuse.

Some are there to fill a gap in their schedules; some, out of a newcomer's curiosity; and others, perhaps out of habit. Yet, like you, most group members keep coming because they enjoy stories and have learned to recognize the written word as both a window and a mirror, continually surprising us with a picture of our own struggles and follies glimpsed through the window of other lives.

This week, we are looking through the window provided by author Richard Wright and see him as a nineteen-year-old black man in 1927, trying to get books from the public library in Memphis, Tennessee.

We watch Wright in the office where he works, considering which of his white co-workers to ask for help in getting the books he wants. Because blacks are not permitted to have library cards in 1927 Memphis, Wright has to find someone he can trust to ask for the loan of his card and a note authorizing him to collect the desired books. He has to identify which of his co-workers will understand and not be threatened by his desire to acquire knowledge that can narrow the gap between Wright and the white establishment.

As one of our group members puts it, he has to find someone who does not want to keep Wright a prisoner of the "slave mentality." The author also needs a confederate who sincerely believes in his capacity to read and learn, who will not dismiss his ambition as an unrealistic expectation, and who will refrain from paternalistic warnings to be careful what he reads because it might addle his brain.

Wright chooses wisely, and with the library card provided by his ally and his own quick thinking, he convinces a suspicious librarian to lend him the books he wants. What he reads inspires and encourages him, giving him a glimpse of a larger life that he had scarcely imagined. His newfound knowledge is both a blessing and a curse, offering him at once the hope of a better life and the challenge of having to do something different in order to get what he begins to dream that he might one day have.

For the author, the choice is clear though by no means easy. He can remain in the South and live out the role of the genial slave pretending to be content while the established order limits his opportunities and tramples his dignity. He can turn his hatred of his oppressors against himself and, by extension, against others of his own race or try to forget his sorrows in the oblivion of alcohol and sex. But Wright, who refuses to let others violate his dignity, will not violate himself. His only recourse is to leave Memphis for the promise of a better life in the North and the challenge of unknown dangers in an unfamiliar place.

A young black woman in the group exclaims in surprise that the author is talking about her. Although she has been diagnosed with paranoid schizophrenia, she is not voicing an idea of reference but, instead, resonating with a universal theme of minority persecution. The ensuing discussion takes us from an examination of racial prejudice to a consideration of the ways in which people with mental illness are injured by ignorance, bigotry, and even well-meaning paternalism that sets artificial limits on the extent of their recovery.

The hardest limits to surpass are the ones we impose on ourselves because illness and failure have made us too afraid or too weary to revise our dreams and try again. In our group therapy room, the distance between Memphis of 1927 and New England of 2007 shrinks to the length of time it takes to realize that prejudice continues to do its damage and that extraordinary courage is as important here and now as it was there and then. It has been a good group, but next week, yes, definitely next week, you'll go to the library.

From *New England Psychologist*, July 2007.

FIVE FUNERALS AND A WEDDING

One of the last decade's most popular movies was the romance, *Four Weddings and a Funeral*, about the lives, loves, and one sudden death among a group of young adults in Britain. The film was in turn hilarious, heartbreaking, and touching in the way only the film industry can deliver in a neat, ninety-minute package.

With the recent passing of an elderly aunt, the same period of time in my own life yields the material for five funerals and a wedding, a common enough storyline for those of us in the growing ranks of maturing baby boomers. From the perspective of the twenty-some-things in the film, the age of more funerals than weddings must indeed be a grim prospect. Yet, when you get there, if you're lucky, it may not be so bad.

These were my thoughts as I sat among dwindling numbers of family and friends in the funeral parlor from which the remains of my aunt would soon be carried first to her church and then to the cemetery. I had not seen Aunt Helen in more than thirty years, and my memories of her were the recollections of childhood adventures at her house with my cousins and brief adult encounters in times of family crisis or celebration. We are a family, like so many others, of weddings and funerals.

The memory board displaying photographs of Helen in her high school cap and gown, at her wedding to Uncle Buddy, with her children and grandchildren, and more recently, in the stands at the U.S. Open tennis tournament chronicled a long and full life. Missing were the tragedies that took away her husband, three adult children, and their spouses through a series of accidents and illnesses to which she could only stand by and bear witness. Family and friends needed no reminders of the sad times. It was enough to know that Helen carried on in her close relationships with her grandchildren who were now celebrating her life and her love.

The funeral of a person who has lived long and died well shows a balance of grief and laughter, sorrow and silliness—an amalgamation of all the contradictions that constitute any life. In the presence of the deceased, talk turns to the most basic ties of family resemblance. Snatches of conversation from the row behind me reveal two sisters teasing each other about features each inherited from different family members. One definitely has Daddy's nose, while the other has Mommy's chin.

Cousins whose births I remember from my own childhood enter the room as mature adults with families of their own. Other mourners are second cousins who would still be strangers had this day not brought together the scattered remnants of what we call family. Now enter Helen's brother and sister, my youngest aunt and uncle, and our band is complete.

Complete—perhaps that is what a full life yields at the end. The pictures on the memory board span a lifetime, but every photograph of an older Helen contains the essence of the younger person she once was. This is how we carry our experience with us. We are like trees that accumulate rings of growth containing the experience of the living organism through all of its seasons. Perhaps this is why, when we are reunited with old friends or distant family members, we feel an instant spark of connection that somehow manages to escape even the blurring effects of fading memory.

At first, my cousin and I are not entirely sure we recognize one another, but we instantly feel at home in each other's company. Somewhere deep within the cores of our life experience, we are still the two children growing up on the same block. Her mother, my aunt, is still the high school girl who babysat for me. Our mutual uncle is ever the family's college bound pioneer.

Can five funerals and a wedding ever trump four weddings and a funeral? The wedding side of the balance needs no one to argue its merits, but eventually the weight of the years tips the scale toward funerals. As occasions of memory, celebration, reunion, and reflection, funerals are not without their benefits. Funerals give grief a voice and remind us of our own mortality, but they can also awaken the earlier selves that live on in the people we have become. As much as older people may envy youth, I don't think many of us would want to relive those years. As wonderful as it is to have your whole life before you, there is also a lot to be said for having it within you.

A familiar prayer in my religious tradition ends with the phrase, "as it was in the beginning, is now, and ever shall be." Funerals remind us that our now contains our beginning. And as for that which "ever shall be," it will take more than psychology to learn the answer.

From *New England Psychologist*, April 2008.

•••

MENTAL HEALTH ON THE BLUE LINE TO TIJUANA

Search the internet for articles about the mentally ill riding trains and buses, and you will find stories about people with mental illness behaving badly on commuter or long-distance bus routes and railway lines. One blogger describes fellow riders on Seattle's Number

70 bus route ranting about government conspiracies. Another tells the story of an agitated man on a Greyhound bus who slapped a cross-dressing passenger and then kissed an elderly man. It should come as no surprise that media reports are skewed. Bad news catches the public's attention. Now that I have yours, here's a story about one of the good guys.

My wife and I had come to the end of a long and pleasant day playing tourist in San Diego when we boarded a trolley back to our hotel from an outlying area of the city. As is our custom when we travel, we forgo the convenience of taxis for the authenticity of walking and riding public transportation. On that particular day, we had traveled by foot, ferry, bicycle, and trolley, etching every bump and bend of our route into the very fiber of our beings. It was getting late, and if we didn't make the trolley that was waiting in the station when we arrived, we would have had a long wait for another.

Our chances looked slim as passengers filed onto the sleek red conveyance already humming with the electric buzz of a machine eager to hurl itself down the rails. After assuring ourselves that this was the blue line in the direction of Tijuana and buying tickets from a vending machine, we hopped aboard just in time.

With our triumph tempered only by fatigue, we assumed the self-satisfied expression of successful urban explorers. Perhaps that expression told the man sitting opposite us that we were kindred spirits, fellow connoisseurs of the rails, or maybe he gave the same monologue to anyone within reach of his voice. At any rate, this short, squat man with greasy dark hair, missing teeth, and some kind of identification card hanging from a cord around his neck, told us in a raspy monotone about his day riding the bus and the trolley. He was halfway through his second round-trip of the day between San Diego and his home in

Oceanside, California, a distance of forty miles each way. He traveled by Greyhound bus and was using the trolley to connect to the main station where he would embark on his return trip.

We learned that Greyhound offers a free bus ticket to the destination of your choice if you complete ten round-trips of any length in a calendar year. This deal, he told us, is a much better one than that offered by Amtrak, which also gives a free ticket for ten round-trips. On the train, however, your free trip is restricted to the distance covered by rides you took to earn it.

Our traveling companion explained that he used his free bus ticket to visit Denver two years ago. Last year, he did not get a free ticket because, although he completed his tenth round-trip before the last day of December, the trip was not credited to his account until after the new year.

Lately he's been riding the bus less often, staying home instead to watch television now that he has a roommate who insists on buying the premium cable package with hundreds of channels. The cable package wasn't his idea, but he still pays his half of the bill and figures he might as well use that for which he's paying. The roommate wasn't his idea either, but his conservator didn't trust him to live alone.

At some point, our confident travelers' expressions must have given way to looks of concern when we realized we weren't sure where to get off the trolley. It was then that our companion broke off his monologue and asked where we were going. He not only told us where we should get off but also explained that our regular stop was closed because of construction.

These days at the hospital where I practice psychology we are hearing a lot about patient-driven treatment plans and recovery goals based on individual strengths and preferences. I wonder how my conversation with our traveling companion would have been different had it occurred on my turf and not his. I know I would have asked what he likes about long-distance bus and train travel, what he thinks about as he stares out the window at the passing scenery or engages people like me with the story of his traveling life.

Why did his conservator stop trusting him and insist that he have a roommate? Why does he have a conservator in the first place? There is no end to the questions we think we must ask to learn what we consider important about a person.

If I had met this man in the hospital, I hope I would not have been too quick to discourage his love of riding buses, trains, and trolleys. The psychologists he did meet in hospitals and clinics have obviously respected his traveling impulse or been defeated in their attempts to cure it. Either way, he won, and as I learned that night on the trolley, so did I.

From *New England Psychologist*, October 2012.

FOUR

Our Lives in Community

None of us goes it alone in life. Even when we think we are flying solo, we are forgetting the engineers who designed the plane, the sheet metal workers, technicians, and riveters who put it together, the air traffic controllers, and the ground crew who provide the machinery and support services that make flight possible. The essays in this chapter span the years between 1993 and 2009, a time in my life and career when events conspired to heighten my awareness of the community that surrounds and sustains me.

When I began working at Westborough State Hospital in 1992, I was completing my transition from being a psychologist in an outpatient clinic to working as part of a multidisciplinary clinical team in a setting where you saw your patients throughout the day and not just during a one-hour weekly psychotherapy session.

I had always enjoyed the consultation and support that my colleagues provided when I worked in outpatient clinics, but now the coordination of services in a secure hospital environment required even closer teamwork.

Decisions about increasing or decreasing a patient's level of supervision had to take into account both the risks and benefits of providing an opportunity for more independent functioning. Psychologists, psychiatrists, nurses, social workers, and occupational therapists needed a common understanding of a person's long-term and short-term goals to avoid working at cross purposes with colleagues and to maximize the impact of our therapeutic efforts.

There were more meetings to attend and more opportunities to get to know fellow team members who, in the best of circumstances, formed a network of support not only for our patients but also for one another.

These were also the years that saw the decline and death, first of my father in 1996, and then of my mother in 2005. When I visited my father in the hospital after each of his four strokes and one surgery, it was hard to leave him in his weakened state and drive two hundred miles back to my own home.

Worried and afraid, I was torn between the wish to make the most of the time we had left and the bonds of love and family calling me back to my wife and children. In reality, there was little I could do for him, and over a period of ten years, he recovered from every episode but one. Eventually I discovered that it was easier for me to leave his bedside when I realized that I was entrusting his care to a community of dedicated doctors and nurses. Because I had seen their skill and felt their compassion during my visits and telephone calls, I knew my father was in good hands.

With the medical know-how and availability that I lacked, they were standing in for me. In return, I began to see how my own work as a hospital psychologist gave me the opportunity to stand in for the distant family members of my own patients. Together the medical team in New Jersey and the mental health team in Massachusetts, even though we would never meet, formed a community of caregivers where each of us could be both doctor and patient.

Community also sustained my mother through the progression of Alzheimer's disease that first started to become evident shortly after my father's death. Her friends were the first to notice her declining memory and watched her closely when they traveled together. She lived alone in the small apartment she and my father had occupied for decades and refused to leave even when it was clear to her friends and family that she would benefit from an assisted living situation.

As the disease progressed, she lost the ability to make telephone calls though she would still answer when I called. A neighbor in the same building looked in on her regularly, often bringing her favorite foods. From a distance, my wife and I arranged for meals to be delivered and for a home health aide to make daily visits to help her take her medication. We soon fell into a routine where I would call my mother just before the aide was expected to arrive and remind her to answer the door when she rang.

Once a month, I would drive to New Jersey and bring my mother to see her doctor, a kind and competent man whom we both liked, but even he could not convince her to move out of her apartment. It would take time, nature, and chance to make that happen.

My wife and I had been looking for a good assisted living facility, and after visiting one that we especially liked, we made an appointment for my mother to visit on a Saturday morning. When we arrived at her apartment on Friday evening, we found my mother on the bathroom floor where she had fallen. We did not know how long she had been lying there, but she could communicate and had no obvious injuries.

We had her admitted to the hospital, and her doctor arranged for her transfer to a rehab center when she was ready to be discharged. This transfer gave us time to find a care facility near our home in Massachusetts, to clean out her apartment, and to fill a small rental truck with the furniture and other belongings that were worth keeping.

With our small caravan of two vehicles, my wife driving the car carrying my mother and I behind the wheel of the truck containing all her worldly possessions, we delivered her to what would be her last home and into the care of another community of doctors, nurses, and aides.

When I am most aware of the support others give me, I feel as if I am being carried on the wings of a multitude of communities—family, friends, co-workers, teachers, students, patients, and service professionals of every kind who stop me from falling off the world that they work so hard to keep spinning. Together, we influence and sustain one another in communities both visible and invisible.

DISCOVERING THE
COMMUNITY SPIRIT

When the phrase "spaceship earth" made its way into our language to emphasize our common journey on a fragile planet, we suddenly had a new and dramatic way to express our sense of community. Yet, on an inpatient unit, expressions of community are generated daily in countless, ordinary interactions between patients and staff, riders together through the uncertain firmament of shared perils and opportunities.

Today, as I sit in a therapy group that I co-lead at the hospital, I listen to group members discussing the belief that to depend on other people is to show weakness and make ourselves vulnerable to hurt and disappointment. A patient with a history of alcoholism recounts his failed attempts to substitute the bottle for personal relationships. Drinking, he used to think, hurts no one but himself, and unlike other people, a drink is always there to relieve or numb the pain of unpleasant feelings. Time and repeated hospitalizations have taught him otherwise.

"No man is an island," another group member quotes John Donne, "ask not for whom the bell tolls. It tolls for thee."

I am thinking how I have learned more about community and interdependence in my last two years on inpatient units than I have in the previous sixteen in an outpatient clinic. When you spend every working day with your patients, and not just a fifty-minute hour, you cannot disappear behind the otherwise useful shield of analytic anonymity.

Last winter, as I stood in the snow-slick road after a minor traffic accident, I would have appreciated a shield of any kind. I was too busy assessing the damage to my car to notice a van full of hospital patients traveling slowly around the corner and affording its passengers a good look at the scene. For months thereafter, my car's battered fender announced my misfortune every morning as I drove up to the building housing the patients' rooms and staff offices. Those who had seen me in the road knew what had happened, and others freely asked, "What happened to your car, Doc?"

There was no room here for a clever analytic inquiry into the patient's fantasy about my crushed fender. The only answer that made sense was the immediate reaction, the human reaction, the plain and simple truth. I crashed. I braked when I should have shifted. With all my therapeutic talk about taking control of life, I lost control of my car in the face of more powerful forces of snow and ice and wind. There are limits. The next time I will try to be smarter; the next time I hope to be as lucky.

I force my wandering thoughts back to the business of the group. Discussing interdependence, my co-leader has asked for examples of people working together to achieve a common goal. Someone offers the situation of a band where each member must listen to the others and adjust his own playing accordingly. It is only by seeing oneself in relation to others that a pleasing result can be achieved.

This morning before group, a colleague handed me the hospital identification badge that I had lost. A patient found it and gave it to the first staff member he saw so that it might be returned to me. Interdependence. This small act of consideration undoubtedly saved me an enormous amount of time and inconvenience. I remind myself to look for this patient and thank him.

Group members offer examples of people working together, and I recall a therapy session with a young man earlier this summer. A self-taught auto mechanic, he had been unable to work because of his illness. That day, with his delusions under better control, he was able to talk coherently about important concerns.

"By the way, Doc," he said as I was leaving, "if you tightened the fan belt, your car wouldn't make that awful racket." I thanked him for the tip; advice about a fan belt for advice about delusions. I know a good deal when I see one.

Back with my group, I offer an example of interdependence that has guided my efforts as a therapist over the years, something I was once told and have held on to ever since. All true therapy is a collaboration of experts: the patient who is the expert on himself and the therapist who is the expert on human behavior. It is only when we listen to one another that the work gets done; it is only in community that we are fully ourselves.

From *Massachusetts Psychologist*, November 1993.

• • •

SPIRITS AT THE DOOR

There are still a few candy bars left in the basket by the front door, and a much bigger pile of treats covers the floor where my son emptied his pillowcase of his own Halloween bounty. I step over the candy and climb the stairs to my office to write these words for December, still thinking of all the ghosts, princesses, firefighters, and scary creatures that graced our doorway last night.

Our neighborhood does Halloween in a big way, and the staggering number and variety of visitors highlight the meaning of this time of saints, souls, and spirits when we remember all who have gone before us. I think of a line written by one of our patients, who is about to be discharged after thirty-five years in the hospital, "I am the product of many people."

This line lies nestled on a single sheet of paper on which Fred has managed to fit the significant events of his nearly sixty years, most of which have been marked by mental illness. The line has a poetic ring, and I tell him so because I know Fred is a lover of poetry. Whatever else may have nurtured this interest, he once told me that it was his illness and the problems it caused with concentration that led him away from reading longer prose to poems that he could assimilate more easily. Fred explains that his years in the hospital have given him the opportunity to meet and be influenced by a great many doctors, nurses, psychologists, social workers, and others who have shaped him into the person he is today.

When Fred says that he is the product of many people, he is describing his life the way I might describe my house, repaired, painted, roofed, exterminated, heated, cooled, plumbed, and wired by a succession of specialists who keep it in working order. Fred sees his life as having been restored to working order by the professionals who have cobbled him together and made him whole when mental illness tore him apart.

There is, of course, a larger sense in which Fred's life and all of our lives are the products of many people, and it begins with our parents. Not long ago, I had the pleasure of consulting with a well-established executive who was considering leaving a secure job and starting his own business.

All the available information pointed to the likelihood of success in his new independent venture, yet he was unsure of himself. He explained that the role model of the independent businessman was missing from his family. His mother was a housewife and his father worked as a welder for the same factory in his hometown until he retired. What did they know about starting a business? What could he have possibly learned from them that he could use now?

Earlier in our conversation, this man told me that his parents built the family home by themselves, buying a choice parcel of land on a hillside, clearing the trees and vegetation, and building a comfortable house, one brick, one plank, one nail at a time. He knew more than he had thought about how to succeed at an independent enterprise.

Like Fred, about to leave the security of the hospital, and the executive thinking of leaving the security of his job, we are all privileged to have mentors, friends, and guides to help us on our way. In the November issue of the *APA Monitor*, Dr. Jill Reich reflects on "all the people that contribute to the development of an educated person in general and a psychologist in particular."

Dr. Reich goes on to describe the benefits not only of traditional mentoring but also of peer support among graduate students and exposure to diversity. As psychologists who know that we are all, like Fred, "the product of many people," we are right to study the ways that we can formalize and improve these supportive relationships. As parents, we do the same when we choose where our children will go to school and, when possible, who their teachers, coaches and mentors will be.

Planning has its limits and, by chance, its surprises. My son has a rich schedule of organized activities, but he loves to hang out with his friends next door. Together, they play video games, wrestle, waste time, get bored, and come up with ideas and projects that delight and hold their interest simply because they are original and necessary. I have no doubt that my son's life will be the product of these boys at least as much as mine has been shaped by the friend whose haircut I copied in the fifth grade.

Fred had it right in the first place; we are the product of many people. Our influence on one another comes through so many channels of nature and nurture, choice and chance that the world is guaranteed a greater variety of souls than we will see at our doors in a lifetime of Halloween nights. And figuring out how it all happens may just turn out to be the soul of psychology.

From *Massachusetts Psychologist*, December 1998.

• • •

FINDING STRENGTH FOR THE MISSION IMPOSSIBLE

Sometimes life feels like the beginning of the old television program, *Mission Impossible*. The show opened with the hero unwrapping a small package and inserting its contents, an audiotape, into a tape recorder. As the reels of the recorder started to turn, a resonant master spy's voice described the hero's next impossible challenge. The hero was always given a choice of whether or not to accept the assignment and reminded that the tape would self-destruct in ten seconds. After a pop, a puff of smoke, and a crackling flame, the hero was off and running.

Warning: These mysterious packages have been turning up more frequently in recent months. Don't be surprised if one comes to your home with the morning mail. Psychologists know about these things because, in addition to getting our personal deliveries and hearing about those of friends and co-workers, we are in the business of helping our patients with their own impossible missions.

In the bleak days of February, as we scramble to accomplish our own changing missions, what we know of others' struggles can give us comfort, encouragement, and the will to do what we can to be helpful. This same simple truth makes group therapy a powerful method of treatment and makes our family, friends, and colleagues precious.

With memories of the recent holidays still fresh in my mind, I am thankful for several natural support groups that still surprise me by how reliably they are able to lift my spirits.

Every year since our high school graduation, eight of us have been getting together for dinner on the day after Christmas. We travel from wherever we happen to be living at the time to the place where we grew up, went to school, and forged the bonds of friendship that have already seen some of us to the point of being grandparents. Through the decades we have not had a perfect attendance record, but our "bylaws" require a good excuse for missing the festivities. We come with our spouses, partners, children, or sometimes by ourselves, and every year, we find something new in our fellowship.

This year, I made the trip alone in a somber mood, not feeling especially able to give or get anything from our holiday merriment. I spoke little and listened a lot, and more quickly than I could have imagined, I was swept up in the stories my friends were telling. Little more than a month ago, we were praying for a friend who was about to undergo surgery for a potentially life-threatening condition. This night, passed over by the specter of serious illness, she was beaming, the picture of health, beside her husband. We shared our friends' joy as they anticipated the engagement of one of their daughters.

Another one of our group regaled us with stories of his continually frustrating and ever-increasing job responsibilities that run the gamut from instructing teachers to maintaining the buildings and grounds of a church and school. Our group's unofficial jack-of-all-trades announced his retirement from a college presidency, and we teased him about his plans for his next career.

We smiled with a couple who told of their son's Halloween group wedding and passed around a picture of him and his wife in Civil War era finery. Kids, they'll surprise you every time. Maybe there's nothing for it but to enjoy the show, learn something from them, and stand by, as always, with your love and support.

My somber mood was no match for this bunch. Their stories quickly touched so many of my own challenges that my resolve to stay silent melted in the warmth of our old friendship. We are the generation squeezed between the needs of our growing children and our aging and infirm parents. We look for meaning in our work and in our lives and try not to lose the ability to laugh at ourselves. These are our own impossible missions, which our connections with one another give us the courage to undertake.

Back at the hospital the following week, I was happy to see my colleagues, many of whom had also been away for a short winter break. Before and after morning rounds, we checked in with one another, inquiring about each other's time away. In a small group of five people, three of us spent time visiting parents who are in need of more support than we sometimes feel able to give. One story echoed another as we shared the hopes, challenges, and frustrations of our impossible missions. We also shared the lessons of our experience, exchanging information and ideas that could help us accomplish our goals.

Later in the day, a young woman in one of my groups quickly filled a page with writing in spite of her protestations that the voices were distracting her. "Ignore them," I urged. When she struggled to read her illegible scratching, I asked her to read only what she could.

She responded with the story of her abuse by a family member, her reassurance to herself that she was not to blame, and a statement of how difficult it is to forgive. The story she told was her own impossible mission in life, but it was also the story of several other group members. Even the silent ones listened. You could see it in their faces and in the way they leaned forward and nodded their heads. It was the way I had listened to my friends last week and my colleagues this morning. There was a new energy in the room, and how wonderful to discover, some of it was mine.

From *Massachusetts Psychologist*, February 2002.

• • •

AN UMBRELLA POLICY
FOR PSYCHOLOGISTS

Consider the common umbrella. Webster defines it as a "portable, collapsible device for protection against rain and snow consisting of a fabric canopy mounted on a sliding framework of ribs radiating from a central rod." But it is so much more than that. How much more, I don't think I fully realized until one blustery December day that began with the discharge of one of our long-term patients. For years, this man had been asking when he could go back to his hometown and, on more than one occasion, had to be intercepted at the gates in the process of a self-directed discharge.

Then, suddenly, word came that a bed was available in just the kind of community residence our patient needed in the very place to which he longed to return.

As in a favorable alignment of the planets, a successful discharge requires the perfect coincidence of a number of elements. The patient has to be ready when a vacancy occurs in the kind of residence that can provide the supervision and treatment he or she requires. Government subsidies, insurance benefits, and appointments with psychiatrists, therapists, case managers, and primary care doctors all have to be arranged. And, of course, the patient has to be willing to go. When everything falls into place, there is no time to lose, and so, one rainy morning in December, rounds were abruptly cancelled and staff pressed into a different kind of service than many of us were used to providing.

Today, our colleagues would not need our learned clinical opinions about changes in our patients' moods or behaviors or our recommendations for further diagnostic procedures and treatment strategies. Today we had one common goal—getting one patient and the cardboard boxes holding all of his worldly possessions into a waiting minivan and off to the life he has been craving for such a long time.

"Well, Augustus," a staff member chirps, "you are finally going home. You must be excited." Augustus growls indecipherably in a rich baritone voice that sounds anything but excited. "Okay then, Gus," someone else replies, "it's natural to feel some nervousness leaving the hospital after all these years, but you'll do just fine." Augustus responds with another gruff and surly utterance, still not entirely clear in its content, though some are certain it contains the word, "idiots."

At least our patient is willing to get into the minivan we have just finished loading with his belongings. Never does our clinical team seem more single-minded or democratic as we each do our part in this intricate dance from the hospital to the community. Psychiatrist, nurse, psychologist, and intern lift and stow cardboard boxes in the rain; the social worker adjusts the driver's seat and starts the engine.

Holding my umbrella over the open van door to shield Gus from the elements, I pull the seatbelt around his considerable girth and into the fingers of a colleague waiting to grab the buckle and complete the circuit. In the time it would have taken us to check on the progress of our house's dozen residents, we have sent one of them off to start a long-anticipated new chapter of his life.

My next appointment is a therapy session with a young man so happy to have recently gained the freedom to walk on grounds with staff that he hardly notices the morning rain. It is raining harder now, but he is wearing a hooded jacket and shrugs off my offer to share some of my large black umbrella.

Grappling with issues of trust honestly acquired through years of abuse and betrayal, my patient is happy to report that he recently asked staff for help when he was feeling especially distressed. This act is something new for him and very different from his usual stoic determination to do everything for himself.

As we walk the hospital grounds in the December rain and the hood of the young man's jacket becomes sodden and limp, I notice the umbrella in my own hand gradually drifting and covering more of his head. Whether or not he notices as well, he doesn't say, but he doesn't move away either. When our walk and our conversation are over, he thanks me with a sincerity that suggests this therapy session was especially meaningful.

Bringing my umbrella to work that day was an afterthought. I am usually content to turtle into a warm jacket with a turned-up collar, make do with a simple hat, or sprint to shelter under an upraised notebook. But the forecast was for heavy rain and it was already starting when I left the house. Besides, I thought I knew where to find a large, black umbrella, a Wal-Mart special that I bought last year on the morning of a winter funeral. It had kept my cousin and me dry enough in a sleet storm at the cemetery and would surely stand up to a rainy day at the hospital.

My umbrella did all of that and more. It is one thing for a psychologist to speak in metaphors to convey meaning in our conversations with patients. That's why it helps to cultivate an abstract turn of mind and a good vocabulary. It is something else to live our metaphors. That's why we need umbrellas.

From *New England Psychologist,* January 2009.

FIVE

REVISING OUR LIFE STORIES: PATHWAYS AND LIMITS OF CHANGE

L ife is always surprising us with twists and turns and bumps in the road that either flip us over or make us change course. We set out for one destination and wind up at another. We are always asking why and how this happened to us and trying to answer these questions by writing and rewriting our life stories.

At one time or another, many people enlist the help of a co-author—a mentor, friend, counselor, guide, or psychotherapist. We can all benefit from telling our stories to someone who will listen empathically, who can recognize truth on all of its many levels, and who will not let us lose sight of our strengths and talents.

The stories in this chapter tell of these kinds of healing encounters between friends, family members, patients and therapists, and, in one example from literature, between Ebenezer Scrooge and the spirits who changed his life. They emphasize the importance of patience, imagination, focusing on our strengths, and accepting the limits of change.

I was not long into my career as a psychologist before I realized that psychotherapy was all about listening to stories and helping the people who told them make them better. Some needed more action and others, more development of character.

I also knew early on that, as the therapist, I was not the author. More like an editor, I could suggest that the teller explore a wider range of possible motivations for the characters in the tale and perhaps consider different approaches to solving the problems and resolving the conflicts that emerged as the plot unfolded. My job was not to choose an ending but to help the author decide what he wanted to happen and how to move the narrative in that direction.

Paradoxically, I grew up in a household where books were suspect but education was prized. Education was the ticket to the American dream—a good job with a good income and a home of my own. This was a long way to come when your childhood home was a rented apartment without central heating or a telephone to make contact with the outside world.

Books, on the other hand, were the refuge of dreamers and a source of information that was useless to anyone with any common sense about the real world. There must have been a few Little Golden Books of classic children's stories and fairy tales, but while I remember the stories, I don't recall the books.

I do remember a giant book of knowledge with a fascinating story about how engineers built the Lincoln Tunnel under the Hudson River. There was also an Illustrated Junior Library Edition of Robert Louis Stevenson's *Kidnapped* that still sits in my bookcase. These were gifts from my aunt, who my mother said was putting on airs by giving me things better suited to rich people. Mom showed more enthusiasm for my interest in the *World Almanac,* and every year, I could count on finding the current edition of this thick paperback under the tree with the many toys Santa always left on Christmas morning.

Even without many books, I knew I was surrounded by stories. All I had to do was listen to the adults talking about my aunts and uncles in my mother's large blended family of twelve siblings and my father's smaller clan of four.

One uncle was an itinerant welder who worked for a while in Greenland and died when he fell through a hole in an oil tank in New Jersey. Another was a paratrooper who was dropped behind enemy lines on D-Day and came home from the war with what the grown-ups called shell shock.

My uncle Charlie made his living at race tracks, first driving trotters and later working as an outrider, leading thoroughbreds into the gate at the start of races. Though I met him only a few times during my childhood, he was the person who arranged for my first job in psychology, a summer job in Boston after my junior year at Villanova, analyzing data from a study of the learning abilities of intellectually challenged children.

In the strange way that life presents unexpected opportunities, one of Charlie's friends at the track was a surgeon who had worked his way through medical school exercising horses. He was still doing it every morning before reporting to the hospital for surgery where he happened to know someone who knew a psychologist who was looking for a research assistant.

The job was just what I was hoping to find, a chance to learn what it was like to work as a psychologist and to test the wisdom of my recent change in majors from astronomy to psychology. After deciding against astronomy, I first planned to study English literature where I fancied I could build a career reading all of the best stories, teaching them to eager students, and maybe writing a few of my own. This notion was not my mother's idea of the American dream, and swayed by her tears and my growing conviction that psychology was a broad enough field to accommodate all of my interests, I made the switch.

I enjoyed my summer experience in the research lab but became a psychologist to do a different kind of work. While I dutifully recorded and analyzed the children's responses to the experimental learning situation, my greatest pleasure came from spending time with them individually and trying to teach them simple cognitive skills.

I was drawn to them as people, and though they could not tell me their stories, I learned what I could by reading their medical records. As I examined this compendium of tragedies, I thought about the birth defects, accidental ingestion of toxins, the injuries, and other traumas and found it hard to imagine the suffering of their families when life changed for everyone in an instant. When so much was taken, I wondered about the value of that which remained.

Though I didn't realize it at the time, this question was one I would be asking throughout my career as a psychologist, especially in my work with the severely mentally ill. This same question echoes through the essays in this chapter.

Until I found a roommate and a place to live, I accepted my uncle's invitation to share the stall where he slept with his horse on the other side of a wooden partition. The horse woke us at dawn, and after my uncle rode him around the track a few times, I hot-walked him before settling him back into his stall. I changed into my jacket and tie and rode a series of subways and electric buses across the city of Boston to my workplace in the suburbs. At the end of the day, I got back to the track just after the last race, just in time to shower and change clothes in the jockeys' locker room.

Most nights, Uncle Charlie and I would join his friends for dinner, and the stories would begin to flow. I learned that a racetrack has a culture of its own and that the people who live and work around horses are some of the most colorful characters you could ever meet. So I listened and learned some more.

At the end of the summer, I returned to college for my senior year where I earned my bachelor of arts degree in the honors program with a concentration in psychology. The honors program supplied a broad context of history, literature, philosophy, and theology around rigorous courses in psychological science.

The foundation laid at Villanova helped me gain admission to the doctoral program in clinical, counseling, and community psychology at Boston University. In this way, it happened that exactly one year after starting my first summer job in the Boston learning laboratory, I was back again, this time for the summer, then into graduate school, and, though I didn't know it at the time, for the duration of my professional career.

The clinical psychology department at Boston University in the late 1960s and through most of the 1970s was an academy of stories. Strongly influenced by the work of Sigmund Freud and his followers, the curriculum taught us how to listen to the people who came to us for help with their problems in living.

We learned to pay attention to the words and the body language of the storytellers and to become as curious about what was being left out of the story as we were about the story itself. We learned to read between the lines and fill in the blanks with insights about the narrators' early life experiences. By listening carefully, respectfully, and without judgment, we would develop and communicate a deeper understanding of the person in front of us, and feeling understood, that person would learn and come to accept more about himself.

With a better understanding and acceptance of himself, the storyteller would be free to develop a more satisfying narrative to his life story. Even in the early seventies, this insight oriented approach was not the only way of thinking about psychotherapy, but as one of our wise professors reminded us, the aim of our education was to develop a solid foundation of psychological knowledge and skill that would allow us to use our own professional judgment about the best way to go about our work as psychologists. We had to start somewhere, and we were taught to begin with the story.

Clinical practice taught me the importance of cognitive behavioral therapy emphasizing the central role of how people think about situations in determining how they feel and what they do. If you can't change your situation, change the way you think about it. If you can't do that, then try to figure out why, and if that doesn't work, try a new behavior or expose yourself to new situations.

Psychological research and practice continue to develop new technologies of change, but in the end, they are all about helping people make better stories of their lives. The essay in this chapter "Ebenezer Scrooge and the Season of Second Chances" presents Charles Dickens as a master psychologist, using every means at his disposal to give Scrooge his second chance.

When it comes to chances, why stop at two? According to research cited in the essay "One Perfect Life," what we need are as many redemptive stories as we can tell—stories about how our inevitable mistakes, losses, failures, and disappointments give rise to new and better solutions to life's challenges.

This is not to say that life is or can be a steady progression of triumphs. As theologian Reinhold Niebuhr wrote, we all need the serenity to accept the things we cannot change. Yet, even in the worst of circumstances, there is always some little change we can make if we have the courage to try.

I write freely about God, redemption, miracles, remorse, atonement, and what I see as the duty each and every one of us has to improve the moment, if not the lives, of everyone we encounter. In its most general sense, this is a spiritual perspective that I hope transcends any particular system of religious belief and has more to do with aligning our lives according to principles and values beyond the self.

I have developed my own version of this perspective as a lifelong Catholic, schooled through my undergraduate years by nuns and priests, humbled by my failures, forgiven by family and friends, and counseled by wise and earnest seekers and therapists of my own and different faiths.

TELL ME A STORY

Life with its many surprises has a way of changing the stories we would have liked to write for ourselves, and severe mental illness can be one of the cruelest editors. No one knows this better than patients and their families. The perspectives of these groups on treatment and the education of mental health professionals was a key and controversial issue in a summer conference co-sponsored by the Department of Mental Health and the Alliance for the Mentally Ill of Massachusetts.

There were no surprises in the remarks of the first few speakers who referred to the significant body of research supporting the view that the major mental illnesses are diseases of the brain. For the families represented by the alliance, this biological perspective had to be a welcome change from the competing theories that informed my own introduction to the field in graduate school.

It is not hard to imagine the sense of injury, outrage, and guilt fostered by explanations implicating inadequate parenting and faulty patterns of communication in families as the causes of schizophrenia, manic-depressive illness, and other forms of psychosis. But what of the patients themselves? Does it help them to believe that their tormenting voices or deep depressions can be reduced to chemical imbalances affecting their nervous systems?

I did not have long to wait for the answer. The next speaker decried the tendency of professionals to assume that their judgment about his mental illness was more valid than his own. With a flair for the dramatic and just the right touch of humor, he told the story of his escape from a psychiatric emergency room after the doctor had decided to hospitalize him for his own safety. Even in the grip of profound despondency, he had no intention of committing suicide, and so he hid from the authorities for twelve days until the commitment order expired.

The same man told of how he decreased his medication without consulting his doctor and sought relief from his symptoms through diet and meditation. I could hear myself strongly advising this man against such imprudent behavior while, at the same time, I thrilled to the courage, tenacity, and ultimate victory of his human spirit. The patient/consumer pleaded with us professionals to stop treating our patients like objects, to stop robbing our patients of hope by blaming their brains.

But when one speaker would entreat us to stop blaming the brain, another would follow with an appeal to stop blaming the family. An unscheduled speaker objected to the consumer's position while current and former patients shouted their disagreement from the audience. This was no polite debate to enhance academic reputations but a high-stakes struggle for a practical way of approaching potentially debilitating mental disorders. It was the mental health field's modern-day realization of the age-old human struggle with the problem of evil. Why here? Why now? Why me?

The evening after the conference, I listened to a friend introduce his new novel at a local library. He used the occasion to reaffirm his belief that we are compelled to tell and listen to stories because they provide the connections between the facts of our lives. It strikes me that in this function, stories contribute to our sense of wholeness or what Erik Erikson called integrity.

Those of us struggling to understand and effectively manage mental illness need complex, multi-faceted stories, intricate novels weaving together biological, familial, interpersonal, and individual themes into rich tales with the potential for satisfying conclusions. As psychologists, we are uniquely equipped by the breadth and depth of our training to understand the structure of such narratives. When we sit with our patients in the stillness of the therapy hour, we are there to help them tell the best stories they can.

Adapted from *Massachusetts Psychologist*, September 1994.

• • •

PRAYER TO THE GOD OF MAKING DO

On my way up the stairs to the second floor of one of the quarter-way houses where I work at the hospital, I meet Ed on his way down. I am about to give him the perfunctory hello of a man late for a meeting when his gaze stops me in my tracks and his outstretched hand reminds me why this day is important. Today, Ed leaves the hospital and moves into a halfway house in the community. He smiles and says thank you, but even in his moment of triumph, I feel the anxiety seeping from his hand into mine.

In many ways, Ed has been one of our model patients. He checked himself into the hospital when the voices that torment him began telling him to destroy himself. During his stay with us, he availed himself of every opportunity for treatment—individual psychother- apy, substance abuse recovery groups, and other group therapies to help him break free from his prison of social isolation.

But even for model patients like Ed, the course of recovery is never a straight line of progress. It is a day-to-day battle with voices, self-loathing, cravings for harmful substances, uncomfortable side effects of medication, discouragement, and fear.

On those days when the tide of battle turned against him and he felt in danger of giving in to despair, Ed would ask us for help. He accepted and cooperated even with restrictions on his freedom that we imposed for his own safety. After months of this daily struggle, Ed extends his hand to mine on the stairway and, with a flickering smile and soft voice, tells me about the life he is setting out to find in the wider world.

Over the course of this past month, our unit has seen an unusually high number of discharges. Like a rare astronomical event, a significant number of patients became well enough to leave at precisely the same time as an equal number of placements became available in the community.

Two days before Ed left, Philip knocked the dust of this place from his shoes and moved to a halfway house near his family home. He left with us his aspirations of being a NASA scientist that were pried loose from his fragile ego with the help of a drug to bring his grandiose aspirations down to earth. He left to look for work at the local grocery store, full of hope just barely slipping free from the bonds of fear that could have kept him here months or years longer.

A week before Philip, it was Mary who took her leave of the hospital. She earned her traveling papers by demonstrating that she could go for two months without serious thoughts of hurting herself. She left with a dossier of coping skills and the hope of everyone that she would remember to use them.

Brendan preceded Mary out the door, but overcome by the anxiety that brought him here in the first place, he was back within forty-eight hours. We urged him to make a quick re-entry into the community, and knowing he could return if he needed to, he tried again. Brendan is still in his halfway house and, by all reports, doing well.

Next week, two more patients will leave our unit, adding to an already unprecedented number of discharges within such a short period of time.

We watch our patients go with a sense of satisfaction that we were able to provide an array of experiences from which they could draw strength. We watch with admiration for their courage and determination and with hope that they will be able to achieve their goals or at least not have to return too soon. At this time of parting, we share news of others who have left before them. Did you hear that Gene is doing well? We held our breath discharging Gene who walked out the door after five years, still questioning why he couldn't drink and why he needed medication.

What about Marty? Last we heard, he was living with his brother and working at the lumberyard. Then he started drinking again and wound up in detox.

Leaving the hospital is always a calculated risk. Cures are rarely dramatic and never complete. People leave with our blessing when they are well enough to continue their struggles outside of these gates. But the struggles go on, with the triumphs and defeats that we all experience, only made larger by the hand of mental illness.

The Christian tradition holds that Jesus raised his friend Lazarus from the dead, but we often forget that even Lazarus died again. We don't do miracles, at least not the kind that lasts. We do what we can and hope that it will be enough.

Adapted from *Massachusetts Psychologist*, November 1997.

OUR SECOND ADULTHOOD — ONCE MORE WITH FEELING

Leave it to the baby boomers to find a way of marketing our senior years and restoring aging to its rightful place as a process of growth and seasoning. These are the days when I am most grateful to be a boomer because there are some inherent advantages of being part of a such a large group with a track record of finding the appeal in whatever stage of life they happen to be passing through at the time.

The sixties made peace and public service fashionable. In the eighties, greed was good. Now the beginning of a new millennium features wisdom and personal growth as the main attractions. If the trend continues, we can look forward to the unprecedented popularity of death and dying in a few more decades.

We boomers are a bit like Tom Sawyer extolling the pleasures of fence painting to a parade of would-be recruits; if it's happening to us, it must be terrific.

What's happening to us these days is something that has been called a second adulthood, "middlescence," or, to use another popular phrase, "my time." The idea is that when you reach your fifties, you pretty much know where you're going in life. You have already made most of the big decisions and have lived long enough to see where they have taken you. By the mid-fifties, most of us have found our life partners or are resigned to going it alone.

If we have children, they are usually already launched or about to be, and by this point in our lives, many of us are grandparents. We spend our first quarter-century learning a profession and the next twenty-five or thirty years mastering it. That leaves only five or ten years to exercise our hard-won wisdom in the workplace before it's time to retire at sixty or sixty-five. Of course, more and more of us are opting to continue working as long as we are healthy enough to do so, and with the increase in life expectancy that we currently enjoy, we might even have enough time for a second career.

Jimmy Carter made this point in his 1998 book, *The Virtues of Aging*, but more importantly, he made it by the example of a life in which it can be argued that he achieved and contributed more after he left the Presidency at age fifty-six than he did up to that time.

You don't have to be a major player on the world stage to take advantage of the opportunities that come with your second adulthood. Every day, people are finding ways to explore interests they never had the chance to develop when they were busy meeting the challenges of family, career, or poor health. A man with schizophrenia begins to sell the artwork he completed over decades of hospitalization, an executive becomes a bookseller, and a draftsman joins the staff of an astronomy publication where his work is rewarded by having an asteroid named in his honor. The real reward for these people is the personal fulfillment that comes from doing what they love and perhaps what they were destined to accomplish.

Freud said that anatomy is destiny, positing a relationship between personality and the anatomical differences between the sexes. Anatomy also plays a role in shaping our lives in other ways. We have only to recall those old World War II movies where the sailor with the slightest build volunteers to crawl down the torpedo tube to disarm the missile stuck in the chamber before it explodes and kills all on board. Jock may have been a wee laddie, but he had the biggest heart of all.

To say that anatomy is destiny is too limiting; the truth is, everything is destiny. Whether you are a boomer well-established in your second adulthood, a middlescent standing on the threshold of new opportunities, or a younger person trying to consolidate your first adulthood, it is useful to take stock of what you have already learned and to take heart when life seems too full of pain, chance, and confusion to make any sense.

We may not know what we're learning from times like these, but someday it may be useful. Go back to that time capsule you buried when you were twelve, the box containing everything that mattered to you at the time. It is still there on the other side of the lake, ten paces due north from the base of the old maple tree. It doesn't matter if there never was an actual capsule, or if the lake dried up, and the trees on the other side were paved over for the new Wal-Mart; it is all there in memory.

Open the lid, sort through the contents, and be surprised by the threads of interest that you have woven into your adult life without ever intending to do so. Top off the capsule with the lessons of your later years. Then pick up a thread, feel its texture, test its strength, and weave it into the fabric of the time that remains.

From *New England Psychologist*, April 2006.

• • •

MAPS FOR THE JOURNEY

With her brow creased in her usual perplexed expression, Mary joined the clinical team in the conference room to review her progress over the past month. Today, her perplexity was mixed with anticipation and a good deal of anxiety about a forty-five-minute car ride she would be taking over the weekend with her case manager to visit her family. Whenever she started to tell us about her schedule, groups that she especially enjoyed, or the challenges of living with her peers in the unlocked hospital residence, Mary would return to the subject of her weekend trip.

"We're going all the way to Angstwich. That's far away. I don't know how to get there, but my case manager said we'll be taking Route 495 and then the Mass Pike. We'll be in the car for almost an hour. That's far. I wish I had a map. Is there someplace I can get a map?"

It is not every day that a psychologist has a chance to be helpful in a concrete, material way that enhances a patient's ability to cope without blurring professional boundaries or fostering an unhealthy dependence. But, if I heard correctly, the woman asked for a map, and here we were—representatives of psychology, psychiatry, social work, and nursing—sitting at the controls of a computer that could easily provide what she wanted.

Of course, the computer was there to provide something else— easy access to the patient's treatment plan as we reviewed the course of Mary's past thirty days in the hospital. After the mandatory review, we promised Mary that we would search the internet and print out her map. Actually, we produced three maps: one showing the entire route from the hospital to her family's home in Angstwich, another highlighting the major approach road to the town, and a third detailing the streets in her family's neighborhood.

I was not there when her social worker gave Mary the maps, but I know how pleased she must have been to get them. There is something inherently reassuring about a map's ability to give us the perspective from which we can project ourselves safely into unfamiliar territory, to help us anticipate the challenges and choices that the road will bring, and finally to enable us to imagine ourselves secure at our destination.

In a state hospital where some people have spent decades, maps also serve as reminders of the world beyond the front gate. Before the building was closed for repairs, one wall of our hospital café was papered with an enormous, brightly colored map of the world that stimulated many conversations about where customers had traveled in their lives and where they would like to go in the future.

When you eat lunch with the world spread out in front of you, you cannot help thinking beyond the confines of the small place where you happen to be spending this difficult phase of your life. With a little imagination, names and places you may have only read about in the newspapers become the stages on which other lives not unlike your own are lived out with the same regularity of success and failure, heartache and delight.

Maps encourage us to be bold and inquisitive and fill us with hope that life might be better elsewhere. They may lead us astray with the false promise of a geographic cure or open our eyes to the possibility of making realistic changes in our lives.

A map can be the starting point for a conversation by neutralizing the risk of self-disclosure as it was for a shy, quiet man in the hospital, who had come to this country from China nearly fifty years ago. When a staff member showed him a map of his native land, this usually silent man smiled and began to speak. Little by little, he started to reminisce about the places where he had spent his childhood and to reflect on the changes that had taken place in the world and in his own life over the past half-century.

I have never been able to resist a good map, from the National Geological Survey's topographical charts of places I have lived or traveled to the computer-generated hybrids that let you toggle between aerial photographs and conventional presentations of landscapes and roadways.

I have used maps to plan adventures and, in retrospect, to understand adventures that took me by surprise. Maps of land, sea, and the night sky have all been useful and often beautiful in their own right.

Least appealing are the internet-generated maps showing only the route from the point of departure to the destination. They seem to imply that there is one best way to get from here to there and do not help the traveler adjust his route according to changing conditions. In the end, the only reliable solution is to cultivate the interior map. On the east coast, we know we're headed north as long as we keep the ocean on our right.

Keeping on course in life is even more of a challenge, but there is an interior map for that as well. Perhaps that is the map that our patient needs most of all, but we have to start somewhere. For now, we were happy to begin with a map to Angstwich.

From *New England Psychologist*, March 2007.

• • •

No Shortcuts to Recovery

For weeks, the newcomer to the group sat in silence. Slouching in his chair with his backward baseball cap and heavy-lidded eyes, he gave the impression of being asleep. His muscular frame and impassive expression kept us from testing the sleep hypothesis with the kind of question we would have asked a more approachable member.

Then, one day, after weeks of silence, the fellow exploded—not with the rage that we probably feared but in a heartfelt plea to be understood for the person he is beyond his psychiatric diagnosis.

Remember the *Merchant of Venice* and Shylock's demand to be recognized and respected for his essential humanity rather than scorned out of fear and prejudice against his station in life? Remember that bit of Shakespeare and you will have a fair picture of what took place in the group therapy room—with one important exception. Shylock's mistreatment had fueled his hunger for revenge, and he declared in no uncertain terms that intended to take it. Our young man was just as clearly renouncing violence and asking for our help to keep his resolution.

As this man told the story of his life and the way his challenging circumstances were complicated further by the emergence of a mental illness in his teens, he balanced the failures so well chronicled in his medical record with reminders of his equally impressive successes.

He took offense when he heard another patient's behavior labeled as "strange" by hospital staff and asked how anything marked with the dignity due to the human person could be so callously noted and dismissed.

He told us about a child in his neighborhood with a severe developmental disorder that in his estimation would make him and his fellow patients appear to be exemplars of mental health. When he described his neighbor, he gave us a picture of a little boy so radically different from what most of us consider normal but no less a complex person with likes and dislikes and the capacity to respond to the attention of others. The young man knew these things about the boy because he clearly took the time to look beyond the obvious to the hidden strengths that people so often missed.

The young man in our group told us nothing about acknowledging the strengths of our patients that we hadn't already encountered scores of times in formal lectures, the scientific literature, and in our daily experience as therapists. Maybe it wasn't so much the message that impressed us as it was the messenger, the timing, and the manner of its delivery.

Sometimes, it is not the therapist but the patient who has to be reminded and convinced of her strengths. A young woman who has been hospitalized a few times is now learning to integrate various aspects of herself into an image that is positive, hopeful, and realistic. She understands she has a mental illness but also knows how to identify its symptoms and take action to minimize the chances that they will interfere with the life she wants for herself.

These days, her presentation is markedly different from that of the apprehensive person so puzzled and shamed by her illness that she would spend hour after hour describing every aspect of her being that once radiated health—her brighter smile, stronger voice, glowing complexion, and easy manner that all seemed to fade when mental illness struck. All of the assurance that we felt capable of providing seemed to do nothing to convey the message that she was a good and whole person with a new challenge that she could learn to manage. Yet until she could accept her basic dignity, she was unable to acknowledge and begin to address the problems that brought her to the hospital.

Elementary geometry teaches us that the shortest distance between two points is a straight line, and in our work as therapists, we are sometimes tempted to find and travel that line from problem to cure. Eventually, we learn the limitations of the geometrical paradigm and look for another way of understanding what we do. In this quest, we may do well to emulate that new breed of philosophers, architects, and urban specialists who style themselves "psychogeographers" in their attempt to reclaim the neglected spaces between traditional points of departure and arrival.

If I were a psychogeographer traveling from my home in a Boston suburb to visit a friend in London, I would walk to and from both airports and let myself be drawn in by the landscape and architecture of the neighborhoods I crossed. My journey would be shaped by a sense of drift as well as purpose, and I would arrive with a better understanding of myself, my friend, and the world that we both share.

This is hardly a practical way to travel, but it does provide the traveler with a thorough knowledge of the terrain. This is the terrain that our patients invite us to notice, the journey that they ask us to share. In their shoes, wouldn't we do the same?

From *New England Psychologist*, November 2008.

• • •

EBENEZER SCROOGE AND THE SEASON OF SECOND CHANCES

What I love most about the dark cold days of December is the opportunity they give us to notice and enjoy glimpses of contrasting light and warmth. Outdoors the cold makes everything sharp and clear, and paradoxically, we are more aware of the sun glinting off crystalline expanses of blinding white snow. Indoors we light fires, celebrate holidays, and remind ourselves that anything is possible. True or not, this is something we need to believe because we see too much distress and suffering and know too well the importance of second chances. This is the season of second chances, and Ebenezer Scrooge is its herald.

Poor Scrooge didn't even know he was a miserable curmudgeon. It was always business as usual with never a break for a holiday, never a moment or a farthing to spare for his fellow man. He had what psychologists would call a Personality Disorder, a fixed way of going through life with no room even for the thought that he might be unhappy.

Like a fish in the sea, Scrooge was unaware of the ambience in which he moved—in his case, a miasma of gloom as thick and impenetrable as any London fog. To say that Scrooge was a man in need of change is to speak as an external observer, from a perspective clearly not his own. His clerk Bob Cratchit knew it and so did his cheerful nephew Fred, but except for Charles Dickens himself, no one was more convinced that change was in order than Jacob Marley, Ebenezer's long-dead business partner.

But how do you change a person who not only doesn't want to change but also probably never even considered that change was an option? More than one hundred years after the appearance of the *Christmas Carol*, psychologists have an answer to this question that Dickens seemed to know from the start.

Dickens knew that the first thing Ebenezer needed was some education about the costs and benefits of his behavior and the alternatives he faced. The author also knew that an aggressive house call was in order and the long-dead, jaw-wrapped, chain-dragging Marley was the ideal caller.

Unlike present-day therapists, Marley did not ask Scrooge to rate his readiness to celebrate Christmas on a ten-point scale and inquire what it would take to move him up a notch or two. Marley knew what it would take, and in a classic expression of tough love, he gave Scrooge no choice. Scrooge would be visited by three spirits, and the first was due when the bell tolled one.

Now here is where we begin to glimpse Charles Dickens' profound understanding of the art of psychotherapy. Firmly grounded in the importance of self-understanding, the Ghost of Christmas Past appears with a "bright clear jet of light" emanating from the crown of its head. This beacon of insight would prove to be so intense and searing that Scrooge would try in vain to extinguish it by pressing the spirit's cap down upon its head until the spirit itself had vanished.

By then, the spirit's work was done, and Scrooge had been transported back to his lonely past and the reader introduced to his distant father, devoted younger sister, jolly first boss, and heartbroken fiancée who cut her ties to the man she loved when his ambition and avarice crowded her out of his life.

Knowing that insight alone is rarely sufficient to produce change, Dickens gives us the Ghost of Christmas Present and the Ghost of Christmas Yet to Come, two masters of the art of helping people to change by exposing them to new ways of thinking and acting in the world.

The Ghost of Christmas Present exposes Scrooge to the common life of humanity that he tries so hard to avoid, while the Ghost of Christmas Yet to Come forces him to confront the baleful consequences of the selfish life he has been living.

The happy result of Scrooge's intervention marathon spills across the page of Dickens' tale with the image of the old man dancing for joy in his room on Christmas morning, "light as a feather . . . happy as an angel . . . merry as a school-boy, giddy as a drunken man."

Like the best of therapists, Dickens knows the difference between joy and manic excitement, and he gives Scrooge his time of rejoicing because he knows, as we all do, that life will not always be so bright. Nephew Fred might lose his job and his wife become depressed. Tiny Tim could need another operation, and Scrooge himself might wind up homeless on the streets of London. Any one of them might turn up at the psychologist's door looking for a second chance at life. We all need an endless succession of second chances, and until the spirits come again, we will have to give them to one another.

Adapted from *New England Psychologist*, December 2010.

• • •

ONE PERFECT LIFE

"There is not a short life or a long life. There is only the life that you have, and the life you have is the life you are given, the life you work with. It has its own shape, describes its own arc, and is perfect."

This passage, attributed to the ancient Greeks, is easy enough for anyone favored by fortune, but these are hard words for those who find themselves at a significant disadvantage. It would be hard to argue that life is anything less than perfect if it is long, filled with loving family and friends, material comforts, and personal qualities that help us achieve our goals.

But what of the life that is short and lived in isolation, poverty, and without the skills or the opportunity to improve our condition? The truth, as always, lies somewhere between these extremes, and the life we live takes its shape from the way we describe it to others and to ourselves.

Writing in the August 10, 2015 issue of the *Atlantic*, Julie Beck traces the development of the stories we tell about ourselves through the human lifespan. Citing the work of Professor Dan McAdams of Northwestern University and others, Beck describes a layering process in which we form our persona first as actors, adding the roles of agents and authors as we move through childhood, adolescence, adulthood, and into our later years.

In childhood, the stories we tell about ourselves focus on plot as a sequence of actions. Later, when we begin to set goals and strive for their attainment, we become agents as well. In later adulthood, we add the role of author as we integrate ideas about our future with our present and past. We look back on the events of our lives and shape them into stories telling what we have learned and how we have been changed by our experience.

There are stories of redemption in which we make mistakes or suffer any number of losses, disappointments, or indignities, yet manage to grow in the process. Loss teaches us a valuable lesson, helps us to draw closer to another person, or to shift our priorities in a way that leads us to discover new opportunities.

Sometimes we don't recover, and rather than stories of redemption, we are left with stories of contamination where the positive trajectory of our lives is interrupted in ways that we can't repair. Our lives are complicated, and they contain stories within stories, sequences of redemption and contamination interwoven into the grand arc of our master narrative.

It is no surprise that research has shown a positive correlation between redemption stories and feelings of well-being. Professor Jonathan Adler at the Olin College of Engineering adds that well-being is further enhanced by feelings of agency and the presence of good relationships. Monisha Pasupathi, a developmental psychologist at the University of Utah, explains that when we tell our stories to others, they are enriched by the give-and-take of the conversation.

Whether I am reading an anonymous Greek saying or an article on life as story, my thoughts turn to our work as psychologists helping people stuck with stories that bring more pain than pleasure and tip the balance of hope in the direction of despair.

In my hospital practice, I have met good people who, under the influence of delusional beliefs, did irreparable harm to themselves and others. When they recover their sanity with the help of proper medication and treatment, they are often left with the desolation of shame, guilt, and hopelessness. How is this the Greek ideal of the one perfect life? Where are their stories of redemption, and how can we help to find them?

For the past year, my wife and I have been visiting a family member in a memory care center for people with Alzheimer's disease and related dementias. These visits have given me an intimate look at the way these diseases can change a life story, and the picture, while certainly bleak, is not without its redemptive motifs.

The facility is staffed by dedicated and caring workers who treat the residents with respect and structure the environment to provide optimal levels of stimulation and opportunities for meaningful social interaction. Over the time we have been visiting, we have come to know many of the residents and their families as we shared our stories in formal meetings and casual conversations.

We have learned not to test our loved ones by asking them what and whom they remember but simply to be present, to join them in the moment, and to respond, not to their often-jumbled memories, but to the emotional tone of their message. As psychologists, we do this with our patients every day, but it takes practice with a family member or a friend.

In a room filled with accomplished men and women torn from the moorings of time and place, I scan their faces and wonder what stories they are telling themselves. One says she is looking for her lost husband. Another shouts at whatever demons he is fighting at the moment. Most are placid or asleep. Staff and visitors bring food, magazines, a gentle hand, a warm smile—the simple gift of their presence. They listen and tell the stories their loved ones are no longer able to tell for themselves. I like to think that the Greek ideal of the perfect life is here even in this room of fractured stories, that redemption is still within reach, and that we bring it to one another.

From *New England Psychologist*, July 2016.

SIX

HOW WE COPE

We all have our favorite ways to cope, and the essays in this chapter describe some of mine: thinking differently about potentially stressful situations, using humor, nourishing passion and enthusiasm, and mustering courage and patience for the unpredictable process of life. While we need our principles and values to guide us on our journey, abstract ideals have to be tested, given form, and made our own in the countless interactions, routines, and challenges of daily experience.

Work and family are our best teachers, the two great arenas where we learn who we are by trying new things, making mistakes, enjoying some successes, and finding out what matters most in our lives.

Even under the best of circumstances, it is never easy to balance work and family life. If I have managed to do this at all, the credit belongs to my wife, Dayle, who found a way to be a full-time mom to our two children while working part-time as a teacher. To have more time with our children, she stopped working until they started school. She did this twice because our daughter, Christine, is nine years older than our son, Matthew. When Matthew started school, Dayle changed jobs for a part-time schedule, closer to home. Her flexibility left me free to follow a more traditional schedule, and the best part of my day was always coming home to her and the children after my last appointment was over. On most days, I was home early enough to play with the children while Dayle made supper, followed by helping with homework, more play, and our bedtime rituals of baths, stories, and nighttime prayers.

By today's standards, the form of our family life was very traditional. It was not better or worse than other arrangements that parents make to balance career and children. Working moms and stay-at-home dads, day care, nannies, babysitting help from grandparents—these and other creative solutions all have their place in a family's efforts to meet the economic, social, and personal needs of its members. At least since the second half of the last century, even the structure of family has been changing with the open celebration of same-sex and single-parent households and the recognition that, at its core, family is whomever we invite into our lives to share our most personal moments of joy and sorrow.

While my own family is traditional in structure and form, the substance of our lives is as different as any family's is from any other's. We are four people of two generations, each of us trying to understand and maximize the benefits of our unique genetic inheritance, personal history, and life circumstances to help one other become the people we were meant to be.

The Greek ideal of the one perfect life, Erik Erikson's goal of integrity, and what Erasmus calls happiness—the wish to be who you are—is more than a personal goal. It is our wish for one another. It is a wish that has to withstand the challenges of the differences that can so easily keep us apart, and when this happens, family life can be filled with tension, stress, and conflict. We have had our share of that as well. I only hope I have learned as much from the challenges as I have from the opportunities.

The essays that follow are reflections on the lessons I learned in my family and professional life. For the most part, they are things that I knew in my head but not in my bones until I tried to live them. Stay present in the moment. Seize and create opportunities for yourself and others. Appreciate how lucky you are when things turn out the way you had hoped. Be gentle with one another. Pay attention to beauty and grace, and every day, find something that makes you smile.

STAYING ON THE RIGHT TRACK

As much as I try to leave my office behind at the end of the day, some habits die hard. Although Freud warned us that "sometimes a cigar is just a cigar," it isn't easy for me to ignore the meaning behind the behavior, especially when the behavior is not my own. But sometimes insight and self-awareness, often so hard won in psychotherapy, come unbidden in the small rhythms of daily living.

This happens to me as to when I spend time in the study with my son, Matthew, operating a set of electric trains that I had bought before he was born. Make no mistake about it, the trains were for me—a purchase made by a grown man visiting London and bringing home a miniature version of the English countryside to flourish in a corner of the den. As an infant nestling in my arms, Matthew seemed to be calmed by the electric hum of the trains as they approached and receded in a reassuring cadence. His curious eyes followed the regular motion of the busy engines and cars. Months later, Matthew would grasp the edge of this flat world and pull himself to a standing position like a giant surveying his domain.

When he started to talk, Matthew began requesting different combinations of engines and cars and soon made his own attempts to manipulate and rearrange the order of rolling stock. At two, he showed more interest in the transformer and its magical red lever that somehow made the trains start, stop, and go at different speeds. He became fascinated by crashes, which he freely staged with his own sturdier wooden trains but obediently only talked about with Dad's more fragile electric railway. Gradually, Matthew's interest shifted to the enjoyment of the smooth, continuous motion of increasingly longer trains.

As I watched these changes, it became clear to me that my son's own developmental needs and challenges were reflected in the way he played with the trains at different ages. When he was eighteen months old and still learning to relate to the important people in his life, Matthew wanted to couple, uncouple, and re-arrange engines and cars the same way he regularly attached and detached himself to and from family members every day.

As a two-year-old struggling to control his body and his emotions, he focused on the idea of crashing and the wonderful lever that governed the movement of the trains. By three, Matthew was negotiating the physical world as smoothly as the trains whose fast, continuous motion he now enjoyed.

I wondered about my own fascination with the model railroad. Could it be that a grown man also had developmental needs and challenges that found expression in the creation of a miniature world where time stood still and everything could be easily controlled? At what is optimistically called mid-life, I found myself remembering a different train that rolled past me as a boy of ten, waiting on a subway platform just across the Brooklyn Bridge from Manhattan.

It was late afternoon, and my mother and I were nearing the end of the trip from our home in New Jersey to visit my aunt, uncle, and cousins for the weekend. To an only child from a small factory town, the chance to be with other children in a place as exciting and exotic as Brooklyn was pure magic, and on Friday afternoon, it seemed like the magic would last forever.

Sunday evening seemed an eternity away until I caught sight of the train on the opposite track, leaving Brooklyn and sadly reminding me that there is an end to everything. At that moment, with my whole life ahead of me, I knew that it would not always be so. I cannot say for certain when or even if I have yet crossed over onto the opposite platform and boarded the inbound train of my life. I believe the crossing happens gradually and that I was protesting against it when I bought my electric train and began to build a world free of unpleasant surprises in my den.

As we sit at the controls, my son and I have much in common. With each passing day, I see him finding other ways to have an effect on his world just as I have done. Still, if he ever buys an electric train when he reaches middle age, I just might understand why.

From *Massachusetts Psychologist*, October 1993.

• • •

SNOW DOC COMES CLEAN

My name is Alan and I am a snow lover. There, I've said it and I feel much better. I always do even though I run the risk of alienating the not so silent majority of snow haters. To make this admission in print is foolhardy at best and, at worst, an act of enormous self-destructive potential. Yet, as I sit at my desk, looking out the window at snow that has been falling for three days, I am seized by the strong compulsion to come out of the closet. If you're wondering why a psychologist is so obsessed with snow, please bear with me.

It is ten o'clock Saturday, and I have been awake since seven. I have already cleaned off the cars and shoveled the driveway. During another storm earlier this week, I followed the same routine and then took up the challenge of driving to work on nearly impassable roads. Like all snow lovers, I am energized by these storms, and this energy is one of the most obvious of our identifying characteristics.

The only other arrival at my worksite during the weekday storm was my colleague who has an equally severe affliction. One day we discovered that we share a telltale sign of advanced "snowphilia"—the habit of keeping a ruler near the door to measure snowfall amounts. In this regard, my condition has begun to affect my family with the disappearance of a number of perfectly good rulers. Luckily, my daughter has an understanding geometry teacher, and my wife's artistic skills give her many interesting alternatives to straight lines.

Besides the peculiar use of school supplies and the extra bounce in our steps when the snowflakes fly, we snow lovers can be spotted by our strained attempts to empathize with our snow hating friends and neighbors.

We solemnly nod our heads in agreement when a young and vigorous associate moans about news reports of an approaching blizzard. We may even repeat some of the old saws about the bad weather in New England or the advantages of living in the South. But, sooner or later, we give ourselves away, if not by impulsively blurting out the truth, then surely by more subtle signs. There is a crystalline twinkle in our eyes and a lilt in our voices when we ask, "How much snow did they say we are going to get?"

Even if we escape detection by associates less favorably disposed to snow, we instantly recognize one another even before a word is spoken. By sampling all of the television weather reports during a snowstorm, snow lovers will quickly discover which meteorologists share their passion.

In spite of what they say, their excitement is written all over their faces, and as soon as we know who they are, they're the only ones we watch. Do snow loving meteorologists really predict higher snowfall amounts than their snow hating counterparts, or does it just seem that way? Now there's an idea for a doctoral dissertation on observer bias! Well, now that I've slipped into psychology talk, I might as well keep going.

What I really had in mind is the idea that our attitudes and behavior around snow can serve as a model for managing stress. Just think about it. Where can you find a more benign yet challenging stressor than in a New England snowstorm? Sure, shoveling is strenuous, and driving can be a nightmare, but alternative solutions are readily available in the form of a hired plow, public transportation, or an unexpected vacation day to collect your thoughts.

Hans Selye, a pioneering researcher on the effects of stress, told us years ago that, when it comes to stress, none at all is impossible, too much is dangerous, and just enough is just right. When it comes down to it, I would rather fight a snowstorm than a fire, flood, or devastating illness.

The psychologist Arnold Lazarus introduced a paradigm for understanding the factors contributing to stress as well as measures that can be taken to alleviate it. Lazarus' acronym BASIC IDE captures important categories of experience that we can manipulate to manage the stress in our lives. Applying this model to a snowstorm gives us the following: Behavior (Buy a shovel and dig), Affect (Smile and think about all the fun you can have sledding, skiing, building a snowman), Sensory Experience (You have to admit, it is pretty), Imagery (Remember the snows of your youth), Cognition (This is an opportunity to be enjoyed, not a disaster to be endured), Interpersonal (Buy two shovels and dig with a friend), Diet and exercise (Eat what you want and then dig), Environment (Hey, what do you expect? This is New England after all).

Well, I don't expect that I've made any converts to my point of view but this was fun to write. Snow loving and hating are probably intractable attitudes, and perhaps biological psychiatry will soon find the gene responsible.

And just in case the professional climate for psychologists doesn't improve, keep me in mind. I do driveways.

Adapted from *Massachusetts Psychologist*, February 1994.

• • •

THE RIGHT STUFF

Psychologists have long taken an interest in material objects. We want to know why people collect or hoard things, why some folks are excited by certain kinds of things, and how things can be useful in soothing us when we are separated from the important people in our lives.

Tonight, however, my interest in the world of material objects is more practical than psychological or academic. I am wondering how to get over, through, or around the assortment of things blocking the way to my desk.

The door to the study is barred by two leaves from our dining room table, a pile of my wife's art materials, four plastic bags filled with clothes going back to my high school years, a basket of unmatched socks (if I could only find the other basket), two boxes of books, a portable vacuum cleaner, and an extension phone that I swear I have never seen before. In a word, stuff.

Seeing it all crammed together in a small space while we are bringing in some new furniture, more stuff, to contain it induces claustrophobia. I begin to feel that I am being choked by stuff that has been silently accumulating around me, oozing from the darkest corners of closets as I slept, blissfully unaware of the quietly advancing tide of stuff.

Today, a patient told me that in a fit of guilt about how she behaved when she was psychotic, she started throwing away her stuff last night. In the cold light of morning and clearer thinking, she now regretted having discarded certain pieces of clothing.

A plastic bag falls open at my feet, and out tumbles a musty, shrunken, green T-shirt commemorating the Boston Celtics' 1984 NBA championship. Will I, like my patient, regret throwing this away? In the excitement of the Celtics' eleventh-hour victory, this shirt became an instant symbol, a reminder and ticket of admission to a community-wide victory party. Now part of the nameless, faceless sea of stuff, it was once a thing of importance.

In his best-selling book *Care of the Soul,* psychotherapist Thomas Moore speaks of the *anima mundi* or "soul of the world." This idea offers an intriguing alternative to projection as a means of accounting for our intuitive belief that things are alive. It may also explain why I am feeling displaced and intimidated by the new furniture that has invaded my room. Never mind that I bought it, that it would not be here at all if I did not want it to be. Maybe it comes down to the simple fact that the furniture is bigger than I am. It bullies me by its sheer bulk, inspiring a take-off on the old joke, "Where does a six-foot triple dresser go? Anywhere it wants to."

Of course, this is irrational, but the furniture, which has forced my other stuff temporarily out of hiding and into a barricade around me and my desk, seems at this point to be an intruder.

The dresser and the other pieces that will join it tomorrow have not yet, in Moore's sense, revealed their individuality as unique objects or things. I am still waiting to discover their souls, and until I do, they will remain simply stuff.

Here is where I have to be careful not to send all of this new stuff back to the store. The mover had to leave one piece of furniture at the foot of the stairs because it was too big to clear the banister. Of course, a carpenter can solve the problem by removing and later replacing the banister. This strikes me as a lot of trouble to go to for something that still hasn't showed me its soul.

But with equal parts of vision, imagination, and faith, I can anticipate not only the usefulness but also the beauty of the new furniture, its ability to inspire appreciation for the skill of the craftsman who fashioned it, and its future role as an organic part of our family's life. I can begin to glimpse its soul.

That settles it; the furniture stays. So do the other things whose souls, still vibrating in tune with my own, lift them above the level of the stuff crowding the room. As for the rest of it, it's off to the town dump. Mercifully, this is not my childhood dump's vast expanse of decomposing stuff, presided over by a man on a tractor with a cigar in his mouth and a seagull on his shoulder. Today's dump is an upscale park with benches for picnic lunches, recycling areas, and a dump librarian who will search for any book you may wish to find. It is a resting place for the hidden or forgotten souls of things.

From *Massachusetts Psychologist*, November 1994.

A COMET'S GIFT

Paying attention to beauty and grace is more than a luxury or an option in life. There are times when it can be the key to survival, helping us to maintain a sense of balance when life's trials multiply to the limit of our ability to endure.

The poet William Carlos Williams celebrated the ordinary beauty of the world in descriptions of simple things like a rain-glazed red wheelbarrow and white chickens that brought a moment of relief to the landscape of desolation and poverty where he practiced as a physician.

The red wheelbarrows and white chickens of our lives have a way of turning up in the most unexpected places, if only we keep our eyes open. They are the products of art and imagination, everyday objects that occasionally shimmer with the luster of sun and rain, nature itself in its grand displays of sound and color or in its perfectly quiet and still presence.

The red wheelbarrows and white chickens of our lives are the kind words and smiles of our friends or the remembered goodness of simpler times. They are the remnants of those blessings that we help our patients to find within themselves or to create in the process of psychotherapy.

One Friday in March, when I most needed to find a red wheelbarrow, I found a comet. It was making its journey toward the sun even as I was beginning a journey of my own to help my father return to the hospital where he had already spent most of the past three months.

Glancing at the front page of the morning paper, I was surprised by a picture of the newly discovered Comet Hyakutake. There, where most days would have brought pictures of politicians, wars, or natural disasters, a surprise visitor from the edge of the solar system had stolen the show.

Its smile for the camera was a burst of light whose pallid forerunner first sifted down through the skies of Japan into the expectant eyes of amateur astronomer Yujo Hyakutake only two months earlier.

There was little advance notice or fanfare heralding the arrival of the new comet. The press had been burned too many times by touting the praises of other comets, including Halley's, that had failed to live up to expectations. When Hyakutake entered the scene, it was simply there—a fuzzy light in the sky one night where the night before there had been nothing.

The picture in the paper inspired me to find what information I could about where and when to look for this new light. As I began the drive into the sadness and tension of my father's illness, my spirit clung to the expectation of finding beauty in the sky the way a man adrift at sea clings to the hope of landfall.

A good comet nurtures imagination and vision both, and the serious observer must be careful not to confuse one with the other. But for the soul in search of beauty, imagination and vision can work together to transport the observer to a place far from the cares of everyday life. To appreciate a comet, all you really need is a clear night and a reasonably dark observing site. Binoculars are useful though not absolutely necessary.

On my first attempt with Hyakutake, the stars shone through gaps in windblown veils of thin white clouds while I peered through binoculars from the shadows between two buildings. I had found a rare dark spot in a town aglow with lights installed to prevent the ugliness of crime at the price of obscuring the beauty of the night sky.

Seen under these conditions, even a bright comet is not, objectively speaking, a spectacular sight. It is a fuzzy star with a hint of a tail remarkable more for its being there at all than for any particularly dazzling features. Even so, when the binocular's field of view circumscribes that faint glow, it closes out the rest of the world with its light polluted cities, crime, illness, and sorrow of every kind.

Serene and impassive in its transit, the comet graces the night whether or not we choose to notice. It glides slowly, almost imperceptibly, across the heavens, a ghostly presence among brighter stars, and everything fades in and out between puffs of clouds.

For a while we watch this strange new light in the small section of the sky that we have roped off and temporarily reserved for our own private use. The sound of the wind in the trees or the mindless rush of traffic evokes the notion of the solar wind, the pulsing gases from the sun that push the comet's tail away and out into space.

We look as if through a window into another world of cold, indifferent beauty that is at once an inspiration and an anchor.

Adapted from *Massachusetts Psychologist*, May 1996,
under the title, "Something Like a Star."

• • •

THE FIRE BEARERS

Psychology has a long tradition of measuring human traits and abilities. We have learned to quantify intelligence, aptitude, and achievement and to describe clinical syndromes as well as the dynamic forces of mental and emotional life. But can we say as much about compassion, enthusiasm, and zest for living?

We can easily recognize the people who embody these qualities. In their presence, we feel more alert, energized, even inspired. It is not simply a matter of what they are saying or even of how they are saying it, though both of these considerations are important. An encounter with such an individual, above all, leaves us with no doubt that we have glimpsed the fire in a human heart.

You never know when or where it will happen. It often takes you by surprise. Not long ago, I found myself sitting in a college classroom with my daughter to hear a panel of faculty members describe some of the programs available to prospective students. The last person to speak was a relative newcomer to the faculty, though he was an experienced teacher and an accomplished professional in his field of communications. He opened his remarks with some biographical information and explained that he had taught at a university in Asia for the past twenty years.

The professor recounted how one day he had chanced upon one of his students running through the city carrying a video camera. He was hurrying to join a friend on an urgent mission and invited the professor to come along. The Olympics were soon to begin in the city, and the government had begun to level the ramshackle houses of the poor that lined the route from the airport to the sports arena.

Together, the three men rushed to the site and began filming the destruction and the suffering it produced. They edited hours of tape into a short film that was widely aired and was ultimately responsible for stopping the demolition of these homes.

The man told his story to make the point that knowledge must be used to do good, but the impact of his presentation did not come from his well-chosen words or strong delivery. His eloquence took a back seat to the passion and character that slipped through the seams of his story like the tears that flickered briefly in his eyes and the tremor of emotion that cracked his voice as he recounted these events.

The room fell silent, and everyone knew that this man meant what he said and cared about what he did. In that room we saw the fire of an intellect inspired by compassion and zeal, and we knew that this was the kind of person we would all like to have for a teacher.

Our family has been blessed by encounters with other caring and enthusiastic mentors. Not to be outdone by his older sister, our son has had the good fortune of finding a Tae Kwon Do instructor who embodies these same qualities of technical skill, passion for his calling, and concern for his students. We marvel at this young man's energy and enthusiasm. When he teaches his students the values of hard work, perseverance, respect for others, and self-confidence, we know by the example of his own life that he is speaking from the heart.

The combination of passion, energy, and intellect is not the exclusive province of scholars or teachers. One night earlier this spring, as I stood on the shore of a woodland pond on the grounds of the hospital photographing Hale-Bopp, the great comet of 1997, a security guard making his rounds approached and struck up a conversation.

He told me that he came to this spot every night to look at the comet. He said that I should have been here three weeks ago when it was at its peak—closer, bigger, brighter. The man gestured with his arms extended, looked at me and said, "You could almost see the fire." But the fire was still there. It burned in his heart and danced with the starlight reflected in his eyes.

Last month, our son received his First Holy Communion, a milestone in our family's religious life. The choir sang something about carrying God inside as forty eight-year-olds marched down the aisle of the church.

Forty faces trying to look composed and prayerful produced forty different expressions. Each one betrayed a spark of its bearer's unique faith, intelligence, curiosity, mischief, or preoccupation with other things. Beyond any church or system of belief, each of us carries something inside. Carry God inside, the choir sang, but when I looked at my son, I prayed for fire.

From *Massachusetts Psychologist*, June 1997.

• • •

A WICKED AWESOME
START TO THE NEW YEAR

Shortly after my recent Big Birthday, one of those truly significant milestones, a co-worker, who was soon to reach the same point in his own life, sympathetically asked how I was faring. He seemed surprised when I said that this had been a really cool birthday and that it was wicked awesome to be the age I had just turned. Of course, he was counting the years by the calendar (as grownups usually do), while I was reveling in my holiday discovery of how much I enjoyed being nine.

With the taste of Thanksgiving dinner still on my lips and the memory of Christmas and New Year's energizing my spirit, I credit the holidays with revealing my true age. There I was on Thanksgiving Day with a house full of kin gathering to celebrate. The small nucleus of family—wife, nine-year-old son, and daughter home from college—accreted relatives the way the backyard gathers snow. A grandmother swept up from New Jersey in a trough of low pressure, more grandparents swirled in from Connecticut by late morning, and by the end of the day the whole system stalled, as predicted, at the house of a brother-in-law, sister-in-law, and young adult nieces.

A family gathering, even of a relatively small family, offers a glimpse into lives at different stages of development. As people spread out around the house, little knots or clusters of activity and conversation emerge, providing windows into the past, the future, and even into present ways of life different from our own.

Here a college student and her mother and cousins passionately discuss the challenges of young adulthood. An older sister, frazzled by the pressures of the day, prepares the meal with whatever help she can recruit. Grandparents do what they can and observe the goings on with the perspective and wisdom that only age can bring. Some face their later years with hope and confidence; some, with anxiety and dread; and some, with detachment and an eye on a televised football game they recognize for the distraction that it is.

My nine-year-old teeters on the edge of boredom. He would rather be playing basketball with his friends in the driveway or video games in the den. We sit together on the floor with a big box of every basketball card that he owns and proceed to impose some order on this vast and scattered collection. Later, we are hardly missed as we toss a football around in the backyard. And when he asks to play the piano for the family's enjoyment, I am happy to be his stage manager and announcer.

This year, when my son is nine, I feel more like a companion than a babysitter. This is perhaps the first clue that I am really nine myself. Yet, looking back, I realize that there were other signs of my true age all along the way but especially at holiday time. Every year when I read Dylan Thomas' *A Child's Christmas in Wales*, I am the boy throwing snowballs, opening his useful and useless presents, and observing his elders. Gladly I leave to others the roles of the neighbor sleeping in his chair with the newspaper over his face, the old man walking through the snow-swept town, and the Christmas uncles groaning in front of the fire after dinner. There will be time for all of that later, but now in the holiday season, I am looking for magic with my son.

On the spur of the moment, we went to a Celtics game, but without a grownup to call ahead for tickets, we were barred from a sold-out house. At nine you can cry about this kind of disappointment. When you only feel nine, your disappointment is just as acute, but the best you can do is to empathize and try to provide some comfort.

So we bought an official NBA hat from a street vendor. Actually, we couldn't decide which team to choose (ambivalence is tough at nine), so we bought two. And, by some combination of ingenuity and luck, we scored two tickets and cheered the home team to a near upset win in overtime.

When you're really nine, you think you deserve everything to turn out all right. When you only feel nine, you know how lucky you are when it does. So maybe there's something to this grownup stuff after all, and these really Big Birthdays that we all have are pretty good places to be. They position us close enough to the end of life to be sympathetic to those blazing the trail we will soon enough have to follow. At the same time, we are close enough to life's beginning to share its enthusiasm and far enough away to temper optimism with a realistic view of the challenges ahead.

In the end, I guess I'm not nine after all. What the holidays teach me is that I have a soft spot in my heart for nine and the tools of maturity to do nine well. And that's wicked awesome at any age.

From *Massachusetts Psychologist*, January 1998.

THE USES OF DELIGHT

It might have been any family outing, a three-year-old girl and her mother picking up the child's aunt at her house and taking her to a gathering of the extended clan. They might have been going to celebrate someone's birthday, or Memorial Day, or the Fourth of July. The scene of two adult sisters smiling at a little girl in the arms of one of them beside a white, clapboard house on a bright spring day might have come from a Norman Rockwell painting.

To the naïve observer, this tableau might have been all of these things, but at the hospital, we knew the rest of a story that was so much richer, sadder, and more complicated. The aunt was recovering from a relapse of schizophrenia, and her sister, child in tow, was bringing her to the hospice where their father lay dying.

Although I knew the gravity of their mission, I could only smile at the family as I passed them on steps of the residence, colluding with the happy image they portrayed. The little girl in her mother's arms was pointing at a building across the street and excitedly explaining or inquiring something of her smiling companions. The immediacy of delight trumps the reality of grief every time.

This is as it should be; it gets us through the hard times. A few days later, in the living room of another hospital residence, a woman was trying to ignore voices that had plagued her since her college days. She shook her head and blocked her ears with her hands to no avail. Her medication, which had given her significant though not complete relief, had recently been decreased because years of toxic side-effects were beginning to take an irreversible toll on her health.

"These voices," she said, "have ruined my life and brought me nothing but pain."

"And what brings you pleasure?" returned a psychology intern.

Without hesitation, the woman smiled and answered, "My flowers." She had planted bulbs in the front of the house last fall, fretting over mistakes she might have made. Were they deep enough? Spaced far enough part? Did the soil provide the proper nutrients, or should she have added supplements?

The answers to her questions came in the first weeks of May when a warm spell coaxed a row of hyacinths out of the ground. We all took delight in the colorful addition to the front yard of the residence but no one more than the proud gardener.

If the immediacy of delight trumps the reality of grief, then why should we be content to encounter joy by chance? Whether the experience of delight is truly healing or merely distracting is of little consequence compared to the alternative of living with the misery and confusion of psychosis.

Treatment aimed at improving the quality of life puts the emphasis on promoting health and wellness instead of just coping with the symptoms of mental illness. In the field of mental health, these ideas have been championed by rehabilitation specialists, notably occupational and expressive arts therapists as well as a growing number of psychologists.

It is no surprise that art, music, poetry, and fiction thrive in mental hospitals. The arts are accessible to all because the need to express oneself is irrepressible and the means of doing so can be adapted for use by people of all levels of ability. For many people, participation in the creative process brings about feelings of accomplishment, satisfaction, and ultimately integration of nameless and dimly perceived aspects of experience into an enlarged concept of a more competent self.

A growing body of research in cognitive psychology is elevating the importance of our emotions, not as forces interfering with our ability to make logical decisions, but as the essential fuel for the engine of rational thought. Our hunches and intuitions are reclaiming their rightful place as the unconscious product of complex analyses too large and quickly done to be accessible to awareness. Anything that puts us in touch with this storehouse of information can only expand our options for living full and satisfying lives.

Our patients teach us that these delights are to be found not only in creative endeavors narrowly construed as the province of the arts but also in any human activity or experience that arouses our interest or engages our quest for meaning.

The curiosity of a child, spring flowers planted with hope in the fall, and honest work of any kind can provide a welcome distraction from the challenges of coping with mental illness. Remaining open to opportunities to experience joy is not an overly optimistic attempt to replace pain with pleasure. Pain is part of the human condition, and the mindless pursuit of pleasure is the death of delight.

Pain will always be with us, but it doesn't always have to take center stage. While there is nothing we can do to produce joy on demand, we can put ourselves in situations where it is more likely to take us by surprise. Whether living well means managing symptoms of major mental illness or getting the most out of every day, we can only go so far by starving our nightmares without also feeding our dreams.

From *New England Psychologist*, June 2007.

SNEAKING UP ON WORK

Sometimes the best coping strategies are the ones we aren't aware we are using. Freud made that clear in his description of defense mechanisms as automatic and unconscious movements of the mind away from distress signaled by the inaudible tinkling of the bell of anxiety.

It's hard to improve on nature's silent alarm system, but over the years, psychologists have amassed an entire catalogue of conscious behaviors and strategies designed to help people cope with all manner of stressful experiences. In the hospital and the office, we help our patients to recognize triggers, warning signs, and danger signs of unpleasant mental states and to interrupt the progression from contentment to misery by applying individually tailored coping strategies.

To name just a few, we have mindfulness, relaxation, distraction, improving the moment, and when all else fails, radical acceptance.

After living with a broken closet pole longer than I care to admit, my wife was beginning to wonder if I had resorted to radical acceptance of the status quo. Her question about when I intended to make the repair shocked me into the recognition of a coping strategy I didn't even know I was using.

It wasn't exactly denial; I certainly knew the situation had to be corrected. It was more a matter of timing and something else— stealth. Quick to recognize the irrationality of not wanting to talk about fixing the pole under circumstances where we could be overheard by the broken, inanimate object, I suddenly realized that I was planning to sneak up on the work all along. And why not? Hadn't I been using this strategy successfully in other areas of my life? And, if it works for me, then it can work for anyone, and I am morally bound to share my discovery with the world.

In this spirit, then, I set forth the principles of Sneaking Up as an efficient and effective way to get work done.

Principle 1: Do not confront the Chore directly. To understand this directive, it will help if you picture the Chore as an enormous, hulking beast, gorging itself on bananas and throwing the peels on your finest carpet. Once you've fixed the image in your mind, then the foolhardiness of a direct confrontation becomes obvious unless, of course, you habitually think of yourself as Rambo.

Principle 2: Practice reconnaissance. It is important to know what you are up against. Even time management experts suggest that you complete ten percent of every task as soon as it is assigned. This practice gives you a more realistic idea of how long it will take to accomplish your objective and helps you to schedule your work accordingly.

The only thing I would add to this standard practice is the element of stealth. At least in the early stages of reconnaissance, don't let the Chore know that you are planning to do it. Act relaxed in front of the broken object regardless of how annoyed you are that it gave out on you. Whistle nonchalantly as you finger your blank income tax return or examine yet another record keeping requirement at work. Examine the task from every angle to get a sense of what you will need complete it, but do not, repeat do not, look the Chore directly in the eye. Pretend you are in the area to do something else, and then steal as many glances at the situation as you need.

Principle 3: Remember that the Chore will always resist being done. A well-established psychological principle, the Zeigarnik Effect, holds that we tend to remember unfinished tasks. Maybe this is nature's way of reminding us to complete all the preparations necessary to stay safe in our caves before ferocious beasts begin their nightly prowls. Yet all it takes is a little empathic identification with the Chore to realize that it is terrified of being annihilated once it is completed. This being the case, how can the Chore not resist?

<u>Corollary A:</u> Forget everything you have ever seen on the House and Garden Channel.

<u>Corollary B:</u> Bring band aids.

<u>Corollary C:</u> Develop a system that works for you and stick to it only until you find something better.

<u>Principle 4:</u> Begin the work incrementally. Do a small piece of the task—a nail here, or, in the office, a sentence there—even while allowing for the possibility that you may suddenly and unpredictably throw yourself heart soul into the enterprise and finish it in a frenzy. Eventually you will do this; just don't tell anyone when, especially not the Chore.

<u>Principle 5:</u> Meet your deadlines. Just because you are approaching the task obliquely, you are not absolved from the requirement of getting it done on time. And what is on time? Just ask yourself how many banana peels you can stand on your carpet or, better yet, how many can your loved ones or co-workers stand.

Now this was a productive afternoon. The closet is fixed, the newly fallen snow has been cleared, and I even managed to get started on this column. It was touch and go for a while, though, when my mother-in-law asked when I planned to shovel the driveway. Shh, not so loud.

From *New England Psychologist*, March 2008.

HOW TO GIVE FATHERLY ADVICE

Ask any psychologist and we should be able to tell you when and how to have that all-important father and son talk—unless, of course, the psychologist happens to be the father of the son in question. Having missed a golden opportunity last year when my son went off to college, I was given a second chance this summer before he left the country with a friend to visit one of their classmates abroad. To be perfectly honest, I had never planned to give a formal speech, hoping instead that whatever advice I had to impart would have so permeated the very atmosphere of our household that our son could not help but to inhale the values that we hoped he would come to share.

Well, maybe I was a bit more calculating than that. After all, we psychologists know the value of displacement and count on its power to transmit messages in wholly natural, non-judgmental ways. "Hmm," says the play therapist at the dollhouse, "it looks like Billy is giving his father a hard time," as the child patient has the Billy doll lock the Daddy doll in the closet. Maybe Billy perceived that Daddy was getting ready to give more of his unsolicited advice and just wasn't in the mood to listen.

Nevertheless, displacement can be adapted easily for use during dinner table conversations as a vehicle to open the channels of communication between parents and children. "Well, son, did you see that article in the paper today about (Fill in the blank with the hot issue of the moment: drinking, drugs, teenage pregnancy, reckless driving, truancy, etc.)?

Once the ice is broken, parent and child are free to express their opinions about the issue at hand in a calm, rational, depersonalized way. "Gee Dad, I don't know why the kid was suspended. Sure, he was smoking in the men's room, but he only had one marijuana cigarette."

"What? You don't know why he was suspended? Don't you realize the dangers of using drugs, any drugs, even just one marijuana cigarette? I know you would never do such a stupid thing." The astute psychologist will notice that the script here needs a bit of reworking to achieve the open-minded, nonjudgmental yet honest note that the parent is striving to hit. We all get better with practice, and the hope is that by the time your son or daughter is about to leave home for college, you will have found a subtle but effective way of communicating your values and the hard-won lessons of your experience—over and over and over again.

Could this be why my son has the mistaken impression that a fatherly talk would sound more like a sermon? One day, he brings home a guidebook filled with the usual travel information about his destination as well as tips to avoid some of the dangers inherent in venturing into that part of the world—kidnapping, robbery, and disease for starters.

At odd moments over the next several days, we each pick up the book and silently read passages of interest. Now, I think, the common text we share will enrich our dinner table conversation, and so I begin, "Remember son, only use an ATM in a guarded mall because kidnappers and robbers typically attack people making withdrawals on city streets."

Of course, he already knows and hastens to remind me that we both read the same guidebook with the same advice. Perhaps it would be more useful if I had some new information that he hasn't already read.

Could this be my son's way of inviting me to give him my own heartfelt counsel? Has the moment I've been waiting for come at last over plates of fried chicken and lemonade? Apparently not, for he now launches into an impersonation of me lecturing him on life, and his portrayal conveys the expectation that I will speak from a position of knowing all the answers. I start to challenge him on this, but he cuts me off before I can say that he will be surprised by how many of his questions I still share and how many of the answers are so often just out of reach.

It is his last evening at home, for although his flight does not leave for another four days, he is driving to his friend's house in another state, and the two boys are traveling together from the international airport. We wanted to drive him, if not to the airport, at least to his friend's house to see him off, but he clearly relishes the independence of getting to his destination under his own power.

In case he was afraid we would embarrass him, I had even offered to forgo the Bon Voyage sign, the balloons, and the confetti, but he had made up his mind. We see a bit more of our son that night, but we share his attention and time with his friends and his last-minute packing.

In the morning before he leaves, I have one more chance to play Polonius to his Laertes and remind him to be true to himself and all the rest of what Shakespeare recommends. Or I could simply make a batch of his favorite chocolate chip pancakes. I know what my son would prefer, and that's exactly what we do.

From *New England Psychologist*, August/September 2008.

THIS IS THE WAY THE
WORLD WORKS, OR IS IT?

This is the way the world works. You are reading the morning paper and happen to glance over at the reflection for the day. It is the Dalai Lama who says that none of us has the luxury of entrusting his well-being to someone else. A few hours later a patient tells you that he had a terrible argument with his father over the weekend. The old man called him a loser and the son swore and slammed down the phone. Your patient tells you that not so long ago, he would have believed his father and started drinking again, but not anymore.

The way I figure it, he says, my life is too important to let my father have the power to determine how it goes. He calls this his "epiphany" and is feeling more pleased with himself than sorry for his behavior toward the old man whom he still loves in spite of it all. You are happy to validate the young man's behavior and even add the Dalai Lama's endorsement to his course of action. This day is shaping up to be a good one, and all you had to do was read the paper and listen to a story.

This is the way the world works. Later the same week, another patient, still trying to straighten the crooked paths schizophrenia bends her thoughts, tells you that she wants to be the pope. Though you are loath to pronounce anything impossible, this one is clear. Age, gender, and religion (she is an atheist) are all wrong for the papacy.

Just then, as you are considering how to respond, the smokestack of the hospital power plant belches a steady stream of thick black smoke. Your patient, who has been here a long time, comments on the eruption, saying that she has never seen anything like it. You are inclined to agree, but all you can think of is the way the election of a pope is announced. After each vote, the ballots are burned. When one of the candidates has achieved a majority and has become the new pope, a chemical is added to the ballots to produce white smoke. When the vote is inconclusive, the burning ballots give off black smoke.

Your patient tells you she wants to be pope, and the chimney of the power plant erupts with black smoke. Not wanting to add to the woman's confusion, you say nothing and wait for another topic where you can offer something helpful.

If this is the way the world works, then it is no wonder people have so many different explanations of why things happen the way they do. The most common involves pure coincidence. One event occurs in close proximity to another with which it shares a common meaning. Neither event caused the other, but because they happened at approximately the same time and are associatively connected, it is easy to infer, if not a causal link, then at least the guiding hand of a higher power. We usually call this God or fate. In reality, coincidence is the product of neither; it is simply the result of chance.

Or is it? There is a particular kind of coincidence described by Carl Jung in which events occur together, related by neither causality nor chance, but by meaning alone. Jung calls this "synchronicity," which he attributes to archetypes and the collective unconscious serving as a governing dynamic influencing the whole of human experience and history.

He gives the example of a patient telling him about a dream in which someone gives her a golden scarab just as he hears a flying insect knocking against his windowpane. Jung opens the window and catches the creature as it flies into the room—a beetle or scarab that unaccountably acted contrary to its usual habits and sought refuge in a dark room at that particular moment. Jung concluded his story with the simple observation "that nothing like it ever happened to me before or since."

Yet these things happen all the time. Unexpected opportunities arise from the ashes of our defeats. Special people come into our lives just when we need them the most. I know a married couple who met when his tour bus stopped for refreshments at a bakery near the university she was attending. He had a twenty-minute rest stop in a foreign country; she had an hour before her next class and decided to have a strudel instead of a nap. Both got what they wanted and a good deal more.

Perhaps the explanation is as simple as selective attention or observer bias. We find what matters to us because we are primed by our investment of emotional energy, our needs, or our fears to look at the world more closely and see the possibilities it holds.

If we don't see what we want, we watch and wait until something of value appears. Sooner or later, we find it or it finds us. Does this happen by coincidence, chance, synchronicity, or the invisible hand of a guiding power? The important thing is that we remain alert and aware of what is happening around us. It may be true that fortune favors the brave, but most of the time it is probably enough just to stay awake.

From *New England Psychologist*, July 2009.

THE SHRINK WHO CAME IN FROM THE COLD

It's cold—deep, penetrating, bone-chilling, soul-killing cold. This may be a peculiar thing to read when this issue hits the streets on the first of April, but now, as I write at the beginning of March, it's cold. It has been one of the coldest winters in history with snow as far south as Georgia and the entire Eastern part of the country swallowed up in one polar vortex after another.

Last year, no one even knew what a polar vortex was, and now it's just another phrase to describe the weather, taking its place along-side familiar Bermuda highs, heat waves, and tropical depressions. Psychologists know that cold weather, like any stressful situation, is not just something we have to endure but a potential source of new learning. These are some of the lessons this cold winter has taught me.

1) Cold induces wishful thinking and blurred vision. It is hard to imagine summer or even spring when every day starts in single digits. Recently my wife glanced at our thermometer with its outdoor monitor and cheerfully announced that we hit the sixty-six-degree mark before breakfast. Incredible, I answered, it was forty-nine degrees twenty minutes ago, and I thought that was warm.

So we missed the decimal points. At least we were awake and out from under the covers, no small achievement when you're in the habit of turning the thermostat down at night from an almost comfortable setting of slightly chilly to a reading of "you've got to be kidding."

2) Mittens are better than gloves for doing most things in the cold.

This point should be obvious. In unity there is strength and also warmth. Five fingers in unrestrained contact with one another generate heat, and when that heat is trapped inside a woolen mitten, the effect is like that of a greenhouse for the hands.

This winter I have mastered driving with mittens and have even learned a little trick to enhance their warmth. Remove first one mitten and then the other and place them in turn in front of the open heating vent on your dashboard. When you have mastered this technique, your mitten will fill like a hot air balloon, producing a very comfortable pocket in which to insert your hand. With enough practice, you should be able to accomplish this warming exercise smoothly and effortlessly while keeping your car on the road with one mittened hand.

Once you have achieved this beginner's level of proficiency, you are ready for the two-mitten simultaneous warming maneuver. Please use caution in attempting this advanced technique and remember to do it only when you are stopped at a red light and never while your vehicle is in motion. I have also found a mitten to be an efficient insulator when holding a dish of ice cream on a cold night.

3) You may eat ice cream on cold nights. Use one mitten to hold the dish as noted in Number 2 above.

4) There are some things you cannot do while wearing mittens even in cold weather. While you can learn to drive with mittens, it is extremely difficult to eat a bagel with cream cheese with one mittened hand while holding the steering wheel with the other. You also cannot use the push button function to change the station on your car radio. You can listen to an audiobook while

wearing mittens, but you cannot change discs without first removing one of them.

If your reading taste, like mine, runs to Nordic mysteries set in Helsinki or Oslo, you may continue to listen, but you may want to turn up the heat in your car. It is perfectly acceptable to pump gas while wearing mittens but quite impossible to punch your zip code into the keypad when paying with your credit card.

When you get to your office, it goes without saying that you cannot type a psychological testing report while wearing mittens. Of course, you wouldn't want to unless your office is as cold as mine.

5) When your office is unbearably cold, be sure to have an extra warm jacket or sweater tucked away in the bottom drawer of your filing cabinet to put on over the many layers you are already wearing. Let your visitors know that they are welcome to wear their down parkas in your office, or better yet, keep a few lightweight insulated jumpsuits handy for your guests to use. These are available from NASA at surprisingly affordable prices and are also tax deductible as office expenses.

6) Man does not live by poetry alone. On one of this winter's typically arctic days, I sent my son and daughter what I thought was a particularly apt quote by Victor Hugo. "Laughter is the sun that drives winter from the human face." While they both liked the quote, they also made it clear that it was about time for some real sun.

Now that spring is here, maybe that time has come. An irrepressible member of our hospital community said it best in a recent morning meeting, "I am back from the dead. Today, I feel great and look forward to having fun with my friends." So do I in a nice warm place.

From *New England Psychologist*, April 2014.

•••

WHAT WE MISS ALONG THE WAY

On a recent trip to Colorado to visit our daughter, I found myself obsessed by the desire to see the Rockies covered with snow. I had a particular view in mind, probably an amalgam of what I had seen in documentaries about climbing Mt. Everest, a scene from the movie *Lost Horizon,* and my ever active imagination.

In my mind's eye, I am standing on the top of a mountain or at least sitting in my car at a scenic overlook, looking out on layers of mountain tops receding into the distance, each layer smaller and fainter than the one before, with high peaks poking here and there above the rest. The sky is bright blue, and the white mountains dazzle the eye with reflected sunlight. If there are clouds at all, they are thin, wispy, and below the level of the highest peaks. I chased this vision for most of the week we were there and, when I came as close as I was going to get, realized what I had missed along the way.

My experience is not unique, and stories of people looking for the perfect instance of whatever they value seem to be everywhere. Surfers look for the perfect wave, stargazers seek the perfect sky, and mystics quest after perfect union with God or existence itself. The anatomy of desire has long been a foundational topic of psychological inquiry, and every day mental hospitals and clinics are filled with people for whom illness and circumstance have joined to deprive them of what they need or want most of all.

Abraham Maslow represented human needs in a pyramid whose base is formed by the physiological needs for food, shelter, and clothing. Safety and security come next with love and belonging following close behind. It is only when a person feels that he is physically and psychologically safe and loved that he can focus on satisfying his needs for building self-esteem and actualizing himself by cultivating a sense of purpose, meaning, and developing his potential.

I am pretty sure that I didn't need or even want a mountain view for any of these reasons, though the punster in me can't hold back a comment about looking for a peak experience. There were plenty along the way, though each one goaded me on to look for something more spectacular and closer to my idealized mental image.

We landed in Denver after dark and just ahead of what was advertised to be the season's first major snowstorm. My daughter was sure I would get the wish I had been expressing since we made our airline reservations weeks earlier. Do you think there will be snow in the mountains? Will we see some snow covered peaks?

As much as I wanted that experience, I didn't need it on the hour-long drive from the airport at night on an unfamiliar road in a rental car. The snow held off until the early morning hours when I awoke to the sound of a storm rattling the windows of our hotel room. Waves of falling snow passed in front of the streetlights while, on the ground, white tornadoes skittered across the parking lot. It was all over as quickly as it started, and by morning there was hardly more than a frosting about two inches thick.

We were pointed west on the drive from our hotel into the town center, directly into the front range of the Rockies. A relatively low but sheer wall of white speckled rock spanned the horizon. Just when I thought my wish to see snow on the mountains had been fulfilled, I caught a glimpse of a truly massive, solidly white peak rising above the rest.

I was to learn later that this was Long's Peak, piercing the clouds at 14,259 feet, the northernmost of Colorado's fifty-three "fourteeners."

For the next five days, the mountain would be my constant companion. When I was not actively looking for the best vantage points from which to see it better, I was catching tantalizing glimpses of its towering white bulk suddenly emerging with an unexpected rise in the road and just as quickly slipping below the closer, lower mountains when the road dipped.

When I couldn't see the mountain at all, I was discussing with my family the best use of our limited time to accomplish what each of us wanted to do in a way that would bring me closer to my goal.

On our next to last day in Colorado, we met a forest ranger who suggested a route to the best view of Long's Peak from conservation land on the outskirts of a mountain town thirty-five miles farther away and nearly four thousand feet higher than our present elevation. Climbing the last fifteen hundred feet on foot, we passed through stands of evergreens and aspen, encountered deer that did not even startle at our passing, and found ourselves enveloped by a profound silence under a blue dome of cloudless sky.

What we passed along the way was every bit as beautiful in its own way as the majestic view that we found at the end of the trail—every bit as beautiful but muted by the chatter of a restless heart and the prattle of useless words.

From *New England Psychologist*, January 2016.

SEVEN

BEING IN THE WORLD

The German philosopher Martin Heidegger coined the term *Dasein*, literally, "being there," to describe a fundamental condition of human existence, our rootedness in a particular time and place. Human existence is not an abstraction. We do not simply exist, but we exist here and now, not there and then. Why here in twenty-first century North America and not in imperial Rome or prehistoric Africa? Whether you call it fate, luck, or part of a divine plan, here we are. So we might as well get used to it and make something of our limited time.

The essays in this chapter describe how four events of the first thirteen years of the twenty-first century affected patients and staff at Westborough State Hospital and the Worcester Recovery Center and Hospital, the two institutions where I worked at the time.

The first is the millennium itself and the pervasive apprehension that such a rare and dramatic turning of the calendar could only mark a clean and absolute end, obliterating all life and consciousness, or ushering us into a terrifying and uncertain future. The media were filled with warnings about computers the world over crashing when the clock struck midnight, leaving our lives in complete disarray. Doomsday prophets predicted even worse, except for the righteous, who would earn their just reward in a new and better world.

In the hospital, our lives went on as usual, filled with all the contradictions, uncertainties, and loose ends that have always been with us, and with them, our ever-present yearning for certainty and closure. Now surely the millennium would at least bring the opportunity for a new beginning, even if only by raising our awareness that we can remain open and learn from life's ambiguities and conflicts. I set all this down in the column "As It Was in the Beginning," concluding with the observation that, despite our fears about the future, we were safe.

Less than two years later, on September 11, 2001, two passenger jets, hijacked by Al-Quaeda terrorists, crashed into New York City's World Trade Center, killing 2,753 people. Another 224 people died when two more hijacked planes crashed at the Pentagon and in Shanksville, Pennsylvania.

In an instant, my delusion of safety had been shattered. Maybe the doomsday prophets had it right after all. There are no words to describe the horror of 9/11, but in the hospital, something remarkable was happening. Our sense of community grew deeper and stronger as we struggled together to process the tragedy of that day. Staff and patients shared concerns about loved ones living near or traveling to the crash sites, worries about the spread of toxic fumes, and about a more insidious and different kind of poisoning of the atmosphere.

What would happen to innocent members of minority groups if their kind were thought to be responsible for the attack? As we shared our distress and wondered about what was to come, we looked for ways to help our friends, family, and fellow citizens in New York.

We also helped one another. Reminded of the fragility of our lives and our shared vulnerability in a world gone mad, we listened, exchanged thoughts and feelings, provided information, and offered words of comfort and encouragement.

At the mercy of forces beyond our control, we controlled what we could. In the absence of global safety, we created safety in the spaces we shared. *Dasein*, our being in the world, our rootedness in time and space, had brought us here, and we were trying to make the best of it.

Every day the newspaper is filled with stories of people trying to make the best of challenging situations, and when our hospital's astronomy group shifted its focus to current events, we read the news as a chronicle of our common human struggles. The essay "News From a Small Planet" describes this shift and the way group members tried to find and apply the common themes and lessons from the news to their daily lives.

We tell ourselves we have plenty of time to do this until something happens to remind us that nothing and no one lasts forever. When the headlines of *The Boston Globe* proclaimed, "Senator Kennedy Dead at 77," the clock started ticking louder for all of us. We knew that it was time to get serious about the changes we wanted to make in our lives and that, despite our weakness and past failures, success is always within reach. The essay "The Unexpected Reach of Senator Kennedy's Legacy" describes how we wrestled with these issues in one of our therapy groups.

Almost twelve years after the terrorist attacks of 9/11, the war struck closer to home for residents of New England when two bombs were detonated near the finish line of the Boston Marathon in April of 2013. My wife and I heard the news from our daughter who called us from her job in Boston, miles away from the site of the explosions, to tell us she was safe.

We were on the New Jersey Turnpike heading south for a short vacation that would include a visit with our son in graduate school. The essay "Not Quite All Bostonians Now" describes the reactions of travelers we met along the way and one man in particular who went out of his way to distance himself from the tragedy.

At times, it seems that we will go to any length to set ourselves apart from our unlucky, unwise, or more vulnerable neighbors. The strategy is all too familiar and all too human, but in the end, it fails. Our strength lies in the acknowledgement of our shared vulnerability, the acceptance of our weakness, and the knowledge that it is only in community that we can ever truly find safety.

As It Was in the Beginning

By clock time, the group was over. But Amy had been battling feelings of wanting to hurt herself most of the day, and as she rose to leave, the feelings were still there.

She assured us that she would be "safe" and had plans to talk with her therapist later in the afternoon. These feelings are nothing new for Amy, or for Billie, or Sue, who had all shared similar experiences in the group that day. So, when by clock time, the group was over, a disquieting atmosphere of unfinished business lingered in the room. My co-leader said it was one of those messy endings, trailing loose ends and begging for closure. The only closure to be had came from the clock.

By clock time, the year, the century, the millennium are over. But again, this is one of those messy endings. Human suffering of all kinds persists. Yet there is something about the rarity of a new millennium, the very symmetry of the year 2000, that cries out for closure. It seems fitting that there should be a definitive end and a new beginning. So strong is our belief in endings, or maybe just our wish to start over, that the anticipation of the millennium has spawned the expected rise in the number of doomsday prophets. The end is near. The end is here.

Louis brought an unusual request to the clinical team. He asked permission to keep a police scanner in his room at the hospital. Louis believed that the world would come to an end on January 1, 2000, and, ever vigilant, he thought that a scanner would ensure that he would be the first to know. The team considered the request seriously. Louis was at least trying to test his doomsday assumption by gathering information. We thought that perhaps we should give him the scanner in order to promote his reality testing and let him hear the fate of the planet for himself.

But experience had shown that Louis does not do well with too much information about police activity, and so our unit director put our consensus into words. Tell Louis to watch the evening news. Surely the major networks will cover the end of the world. Keep an eye on the television, the director said. Keep another on the heavens, someone joked.

During one of our pre-Christmas therapy sessions, Ralph wondered aloud whether the new millennium would be a time of peace or a time of war. A timid soul, Ralph goes through life like a man tiptoeing across a minefield and, on the locked unit where he lives, there is no shortage of mines set off every day.

In addition to acquiring the social skills that his long illness has prevented him from learning or that have simply withered from disuse, Ralph must learn to negotiate the unpredictable social environment of his often-volatile fellow residents. In spite of a dedicated staff's good record of keeping people safe, verbal outbursts, angry remarks, and intimidating glances are the daily staple of life in the hospital. Ralph lives this reality fearfully, but he is even more afraid of the dangers of living a life of greater independence in the community.

I tell Ralph that I believe the new millennium will be a time of peace and a time of war. As ever, war and peace, love and hate will continue to co-exist and struggle for supremacy. I am talking about conflict on all levels, between nations, between individuals, and within the human heart. As a therapist, I had come to believe in the importance of resolving conflict, of accepting the price of getting what we want, or the price of doing without it. That there is also a price of not deciding went without question. But could there also be some value in keeping the questions open and living our conflicts and contradictions?

Spiritual writer and psychotherapist Thomas Moore calls this openness to the contradictions in our lives "care of the soul." He reminds us that each life is not only unique but also sacred and that we can discover our individuality only by attending carefully to our idiosyncrasies, contradictions and symptoms. It is in this spirit that I try to understand Ralph's question about the new millennium's potential for war or peace. His ambivalence about seeking discharge from the hospital is in part a question about where he can live the most secure and peaceful life. His tendency to think in absolutes and opposites—war or peace—leaves no room for the complex nature of the world and his own soul.

Ralph is not alone in his wish to simplify the world and his choices. Perhaps the irrational thought that the new millennium will be the dramatic end and a new beginning is simply our old wish for closure, certainty, and a world free of the contradictions and conflicts that mark each of our lives. By clock time, the year, the century, the millennium are over. But we have been battling feelings that don't quite fit most of our lives. The good news is that we are safe. More than safe, we may have found cause to rejoice in the messy ending, the loose ends, the opportunities for creative solutions that linger after the clock strikes twelve.

From *Massachusetts Psychologist*, January 2000.

WATCHING THE WORLD GO MAD:
THE VIEW FROM THE HOSPITAL

I was climbing the stairs of one of the hospital's quarter-way houses when a mental health worker told me that an airplane had just crashed into the World Trade Center. I pictured a private, single engine plane straying off course over New York City and smashing into one of the giant towers. I saw the aircraft buckle on impact, bounce off the tower, and plummet to the ground. How sad for the pilot, I thought, and hoped that there were no passengers and that casualties among bystanders would be light.

In the patients' sitting room at the top of the stairs, colleagues gathered for morning rounds were staring at the television watching heavy, black smoke pouring from both towers of the World Trade Center. As the anchorman explained that two large passenger planes had apparently been hijacked and flown into the World Trade Center, the tape of the second collision played across the screen in all of its graphic horror.

The patients who lived in this house had already gone to their day programs in other parts of the hospital where they would hear the news as the morning wore on. We sat in disbelief, asking one another naïve questions—how do they fight a fire like that?—as more bad news about the attack on the Pentagon and the crash of another aircraft in Pennsylvania sifted into the room.

We spent the rest of that day meeting with groups of patients in their houses, listening to their concerns, answering questions if we could, speculating together about what had happened and why, and brainstorming ways to cope with the fear, anger, confusion, and sadness that we all shared. One man worried about his mother who lived in New York and was relieved when he was able to reach her by phone. Another was preoccupied with questions about the thick clouds of smoke and dust billowing over New York. Would the columns of ash reach New England, and if so, what effect might they have on our environment? Members of minority groups expressed concern that they might be targeted for retribution if their own kind were thought to be responsible for the attacks.

Not all of the talk was gloomy and bleak. There was jubilation as well when a man reported that he had just learned his sister had cancelled her reservation on one of the doomed flights the day before its scheduled departure.

In the days that followed, our patients continued to process the ever-increasing volume of bad news about the terrorist attacks and the new war into which our country had been thrust. In community meetings, group and individual therapy sessions, we listened to their concerns. We knew their fear because if it differed from our own at all, it was only in the particular form it took or in the intensity with which it burned.

A wall in the hospital's Day Treatment Center became a showcase where patients and staff displayed their drawings and written comments about the tragedy. "Oh, what hell on earth man creates," reads the caption for a drawing of the twin towers and the Pentagon engulfed in flame while tiny stick figures fall into oblivion. "I am screaming my hellos," another poster reads, "but no one hears me, because they are all dead, dead, dead, dead, dead."

All of us who live or work in this house know how fiercely we struggle to preserve life even when despair tries just as fiercely to end it. One death is tragedy enough, but what can we say about almost three thousand deaths? Imagination fails to comprehend, and metaphor does not apply. The events of September 11, 2001 are not another Gettysburg or another Pearl Harbor. They are not another anything so much as their own brand of incomprehensible horror.

Through the lens of a world gone mad, the view from the hospital is magnified, distorted, but sometimes remarkably accurate. When mental illness condemns you to live with irrational guilt and the conviction that you have been targeted for punishment, it is easy to see the violence of the terrorists as the approach of your own judgment day.

When the combined effects of chronic illness and long-term hospitalization make you timid and indecisive, the unpredictability and impermanence of a world at war confirm your worst fears about life outside of the institution. The violence of the terrorists resonates with the anger of those who were abused, neglected, misunderstood, or otherwise alienated from family, friends, and society.

One of these voices suggests that the leader of the terrorists be mutilated the way she used to cut her own flesh. A quiet man, whose quiet life is punctuated by episodes of aggression and remorse, worries that our country may kill too many innocent people in the struggle to come. A soft voice repeats that there would be no war if there were no hunger in the world.

Everywhere in the hospital, staff and patients decry the violence unleashed on the world on September 11, 2001. Our shared repugnance for the behavior of the terrorists and our shared distress are new bonds of an alliance that transcends the categories of staff and patient, mentally ill and mentally well. Now we think only of victims, survivors, and aggressors. Many of us who have survived this first round of violence wait in line to help our less fortunate countrymen in New York. If the line is long and we are impatient to help, we need only look around to see that there is plenty of work to be done taking care of one another right where we are.

From *Massachusetts Psychologist*, November 2001.

• • •

LIFE WITH TERRORISM: NOTHING HAS CHANGED, NOTHING REMAINS THE SAME

What has changed about our lives since the terrorist attacks of September 11? There are days when I almost forget that anything happened. Then I see a car winding along Hospital Road with two American flags fixed to the hood and rippling in the wind. The car pulls up to the Administration Building, and I am watching a scene from a war movie and expecting Staff Sergeant Driver to get out and open the rear door for his general. But it's just the mail carrier, or the plumber, or any one of us arriving for work.

This scene would have been unthinkable in the summer, except perhaps in the days around the Fourth of July with patriotism on display for the big holiday. But now flags are everywhere, flying from the porches of our on-grounds quarter-way houses, affixed as decals to the rear windows of cars, taped to the antennae of every kind of vehicle, and painted or draped on the sides of houses in communities everywhere.

Caught up once again in the business of everyday life, I almost have to ask myself what happened to account for these changes. Then I notice something as simple as a New York license plate, and the reality of the last three months comes back with a hollow chill.

The closest I have come to New York City after September 11 has been a consulting trip to Hartford, followed by a drive to visit my mother in New Jersey. In Hartford, colleagues from Connecticut and New York shared their experiences from the day of the attack and the weeks that followed.

Psychologists who teach and counsel university students in New York City told of that terrible day when they watched the World Trade Center burning from their offices or other vantage points in the city. They shared their feelings of shock and disbelief, their efforts to support their students, and the need to get back to the security of their homes.

One colleague told of driving into the city just after dawn a few days later, parking his car when the road was closed, and walking through ash-covered streets, past exhausted rescue workers, to present himself at a Red Cross station with an offer to help.

Another colleague conducted walk-in groups for employees of a large bank in the vicinity of ground zero. All of these men and women told stories of trauma, gratitude to strangers, and the role of luck, fate, or God in their own survival.

The next day, I saw New York City, always from a distant bridge or highway, but at one point near enough to see the empty space in the skyline once occupied by the twin towers. It looked like very little had changed. An empty space in the New York skyline fills quickly as other structures, once hidden by the towers, step up to fill the gap. So I drove closer, to Liberty Park on the western shore of the Hudson River where, in more peaceful days, ferries make the short run to Ellis Island and the Statue of Liberty.

The few visitors to the park walked along the promenade and looked over the narrow stretch of water to where the World Trade

Center once stood. For the most part, we walked in silence, but occasionally, strangers talked to one another about what had happened. Where a makeshift security gate blocked the way, a policeman gave his eyewitness account of the attack and his one visit to the site to help with the rescue effort.

Bright sunlight and gathering clouds took turns playing tricks lighting the river and the city on the opposite shore. It might have been a day like any other but for the evidence that something terrible had happened—a crane, a plume of smoke, a ring of damaged buildings where holes gaped in the place of windows, and a Coast Guard cutter lying at anchor in the river—all close enough to be seen but far enough away to be silent.

The scene didn't seem real. Reality was the highway, mother to visit, family waiting at home, work to be done. Reality was doing psychotherapy, supervising interns, yardwork, homework, the joys and challenges of parenthood.

Then we learned that reality was bombing Afghanistan, anthrax, warnings about bridges that might be destroyed, and periods of high alert not meant to interfere with going about life as usual. And life as usual does go on, as it must after any loss or tragedy. The theaters, museums, and restaurants of upper Manhattan crackle with life while the neighborhood around the site of the World Trade Center has become the "frozen zone" where shopkeepers wearing gas masks continue the slow business of cleaning up. But even the frozen zone will thaw, and then what will be the legacy of September 11, 2001?

New Yorker Billy Collins, our nation's new poet laureate, was recently quoted as saying that the events of September 11 "have caused people to look at life through a different lens. The things that are trivial, we recognize as trivial. What is not trivial, we recognize as important."

Perhaps, like Scrooge on Christmas morning, we will re-order our list of what is important and get more serious about life. There are encouraging signs that this is starting to happen. We are spending more time with our families, finding more opportunities to show appreciation to others, savoring the fullness of every passing moment. The other day, members of one of my therapy groups at the hospital couldn't stop laughing. This could have been an example of resistance or avoidance or anxiety, but it wasn't any of these things. We were just getting serious about life.

From *Massachusetts Psychologist*, December 2001.

• • •

NEWS FROM A SMALL PLANET

Not long ago, a colleague sent me an email to say a patient told him he was very happy with his new treatment team including his psychiatrist, social worker, and his own personal astrologer. I prefer to think of myself as an "astropsychologist" (never "psychoastronomer"), but I have learned to expect these kinds of misunderstandings after years of conducting an Astronomy Group in a state hospital. Now, with all but one of our group members discharged and no new recruits on the doorstep, it is time to change our focus.

Fortunately, even in this big universe, our own small planet certainly qualifies as a legitimate object of interest. This interest is especially true in a hospital where people come to grapple with the problems of living and relating to others on this tiny fragment of rock that we call home. In theory and in practice, it is a short jump from conducting an astronomy group to a current events group, and with more news junkies than star gazers in our house, the Current Events Group was born.

Now, every week we gather in the conference room with the newspaper, our curiosity about the world, and our willingness to examine facts, opinions, and feelings in open discussion with one another. For some, the first step is mustering the courage to come into the room and risk the failure of saying nothing or saying the wrong thing. Some may fear the anticipated ridicule or outrage of their peers, while for others the dreaded response is silence.

We leave the door open, welcome late arrivals, and understand early departures. The newspaper on the table is our text, and its various sections provide a wide array of choices for group members to scan for items of interest. Each person finds a story and takes a turn reading, one paragraph at a time, before passing the text to his neighbor. Then the group attempts to mine the daily chronicle of our common struggle for some insight about the issues that challenge people with and without mental illness.

A story about a privileged young man who gives up a lucrative career to follow his brother's example of a simpler life devoted to caring for those less fortunate than himself catches our attention. It raises questions about the meaning of work and the purpose of life. Are we here to gain as much as possible for ourselves, or do we have an obligation to attend to the needs of others? If the latter, then how do we go about being a good neighbor? Can we demonstrate caring and enrich the lives of those around us only by working in the traditional "helping professions," or is all honest work an opportunity to contribute something to the common good?

And what about those who for reasons of long term mental illness are unable to work or even live outside of a hospital setting? These and similar questions spring from the newspaper story before us, and little by little, the world outside the hospital walls becomes relevant again. The members of our current events group begin to see themselves as a community. In our microcosm of the grand stage of world events, putting forth your best effort to help prepare supper for your peers can be as important as negotiating an oil deal to help impoverished families pay to heat their homes.

Stories about hurricanes and other natural disasters reinforce concepts taught in our more traditional relapse prevention groups as we consider issues of preparation, planning, and early warning systems. The sports page gives us examples of positive thinking, perseverance, and coping with adversity. For humor and wisdom both, there is nothing like the comics.

We have never stopped being an astronomy group but have merely shifted our gaze to our home planet. We keep up with developments in the science of astronomy and news of upcoming events in the sky like meteor showers, eclipses, and favorable conditions for viewing some of our nearer neighbors in the solar system.

Paying attention to both astronomy and current events may ultimately help us to strike a balance between engagement and distance with each serving as the antidote for too much of the other. Each day the gulfs between the galaxies grow more immense as the universe flies apart at an ever-increasing rate of speed. Astronomers tell us that in 100 billion years we will be utterly alone in space, but for now, our group draws closer together by sharing news from home.

Adapted from *New England Psychologist*, February 2006.

THE UNEXPECTED REACH OF
SENATOR KENNEDY'S LEGACY

Kennedy Dead at 77. It was not the headline I expected to see on that Wednesday in late August when I retrieved the morning paper from the driveway. Neither did I expect what happened in a group therapy session later that same morning. Perhaps the measure of our capacity to be surprised by loss is simply the intensity of the desperation with which we will do anything in our power to deny that loss is inevitable.

As group members were still trickling into the meeting room, an early arrival asked if she could speak first because she was feeling especially anxious. Given the floor a few minutes later, the woman said that the news of the Senator's death recalled the death of a favorite aunt exactly one year ago to the day. Through her tears she told the group that her aunt did not have to die but succumbed only because she refused a difficult but potentially life-saving treatment.

Two years ago, her grandfather passed away. He was old and frail, but there was no reason to expect that what turned out to be his final hospitalization would be any different from the dozens that preceded it. There was no reason at all save the knowledge that nothing lasts, and none of us goes on forever.

Other group members quickly picked up the theme, recalling losses of their own, but always with an afterthought about how they might have been prevented, "if only." If only he had followed his doctor's orders, taken his medicine, not missed his usual bus, then the outcome would have been different, and he would still be with us today.

Then a voice sounded a different, more sobering, note as it asked if Ted Kennedy, with all his influence, wealth, and access to the best medical care, could die, then what chance did the rest of us have? The room full of people who are often loud, sometimes angry, and always brimming with emotion, fell silent.

What chance do the rest of us have? The silence provided space and time for the question to sink in and for the answer to bubble up through each of us from the depths of our own experience, beliefs, hopes, fears, and goals. We need to make peace with God, an older man said with authority, and then proceeded to tell us all exactly how that was done in his own religious tradition.

Someone else complained that her medication wasn't working and that her doctor wasn't available to discuss the situation and make whatever changes were needed. She was afraid that her clinical team would discharge her before she had found a better way to cope with her distressing emotions than her usual strategy of sinking into a drug-induced oblivion. The woman confessed that though she had been in the hospital for months, she had become serious about her recovery only in the last three weeks.

When time is short, we get down to business, and time is short for us all. The discussion in the therapy room on the morning of Senator Kennedy's death reminded me of something the playwright William Saroyan is said to have remarked shortly before he died.

Five days before he collapsed at home, Saroyan called the Associated Press to make a final statement for publication after his death. He said that he always knew that everyone has to die, but that he always thought an exception would somehow be made for him. "Now what?" the dying playwright asked when he knew his time had come.

Saroyan's question echoing down through the years caught up with us in the therapy room on the day the Senator died. We knew Mr. Kennedy was dying, that his time was short, yet we were surprised nonetheless. Like Saroyan, did we really think an exception would be made in the case of this powerful scion of America's most visible family over the last half century? If that's what we expected, it took only four words in the morning paper to disabuse us of our irrational notion: Kennedy Dead at 77.

Face to face with our own limited time, we could only repeat, "Now what?" One group member surfaced briefly from a silent, nodding daydream to say that the hospital was a beautiful place and that he would be sorry when it closed. Another ending in the room with us since the plan was announced weeks ago was back to claim our attention. It had never really left. The daydreamer said he tries to enjoy every minute.

Another group member, caught in the grip of substance abuse, despaired that he could ever get himself straight before he had to leave. He confessed that he was at the low point of his life, and others echoed the sentiment. What good was even a limited amount of time if it wasn't enough to make up for the years that had been squandered?

The early reports of Kennedy's death were accompanied by the usual questions about his legacy. In this context, the themes of human frailty, failure, and recovery emerged repeatedly and were amplified in the days and weeks that followed. We all want our lives to follow a steadily upward trajectory, but reality has other ideas. Illness, loss, and bad choices can send us plummeting to the bottom, but like the Senator, we can work our way up by new and unimagined routes to unexpected heights. It is unlikely that Senator Kennedy aspired to be a role model for a handful of men and women in a state hospital therapy group. Some would say that his character was not strong enough to merit the status of role model at all. But on the morning we learned the Senator was dead at 77, we needed his weakness as much as his strength to remind us to make the most of what time we have left.

From *New England Psychologist*, October 2009.

NOT QUITE ALL BOSTONIANS NOW

I learned about the marathon bombings somewhere on the New Jersey Turnpike when our daughter, who lives and works in Boston, called to say that she was safe. It was an odd way to check in, but we assured her that we were safe as well and asked what else was new. Then out came the story that would have us transfixed for the rest of the week as it held the attention of the entire Boston area, the nation, and the world. Whether you were standing along the marathon route as we usually did or traveling, there was nowhere to hide from the impact of terror at an international event. On the third Monday in April, it seems that everyone knows someone who comes to Boston.

In the days that followed, expressions of solidarity with the bombing victims poured in from all quarters. The *Globe* ran an article entitled "All Bostonians Now," and even our archrivals on the baseball diamond, the New York Yankees, sang the Red Sox anthem, *Sweet Caroline*, in the House that Ruth Built. Not everyone, however, was so quick to identify with the hometown crowd as we were soon to learn.

After gathering the scant details then available from our daughter, we turned on the car radio for more information and then pulled into the next rest stop. Groups of people stood together around television screens suspended from the ceiling, all tuned to the news and all the news the same. As the runners approached the finish line, the noise of the first explosion, followed shortly the second, drowned out the cheering crowd. The barricades along the route toppled like a line of cards, smoke billowed into a clear spring sky, and an older runner caught by the blast fell over on his side.

We would see this footage over and over again in the days and weeks to come and other images too. Now there was only this, along with the drone of reporters and commentators as shocked and puzzled as the rest of us.

Seeing your home attacked when you are on the road brings a special kind of horror, and we could not help but give it voice. That's where we live, we said to no one in particular and to anyone in that small band of television gawkers that might care to listen. Not me, replied a man standing next to us. I live in, and here he named a suburb only a little farther away from ground zero than our own bedroom community. Well no, we said, we don't live in the city of Boston either, but this is still our home. Our neighbor took that as his cue to scold us, to tell us that our home is not in danger, and that he lives in his suburb in order to avoid precisely the kind of dangers that cities breed.

As the days stretched into weeks and citizens of the world tripped over themselves to identify with Boston, I could not stop thinking about this man's determination to run the other way. It would have been easy to dismiss him as an arrogant snob, but that's not what psychologists do. We are always trying to figure out what makes people tick, what motivates people to behave in certain ways, and how there can be so many different reactions to the same event.

This one was easy, and there was no shortage of precedents to account for the man's behavior. The first one to come to mind was the idea of the "right stuff" that Tom Wolfe so memorably described in his story of America's first seven astronauts. All of these men were former jet pilots who courted danger on a daily basis and regularly lost members of their bold fraternity. To protect themselves from experiencing the full extent of their vulnerability, the pilots explained fatalities as a matter of not having the right stuff. As long as a man believed that he had the right stuff that his unlucky comrade lacked, he could maintain the illusion that nothing bad could happen to him.

Perhaps my neighbor from his protected suburb thought of his right stuff as superior judgment that would keep him away from places where bombs were likely to explode. He might have been a modern-day Prospero from Poe's *The Masque of the Red Death*, the prince who retreats with his friends to an impregnable abbey to hide from the plague that eventually crashes the party.

Stories like this exist because we all struggle with the vulnerability that makes us human. Sometimes we distance ourselves from the people, places, and labels that define our membership in groups of the especially disadvantaged or challenged. The hospital where I work is filled with people who have a slight case of schizophrenia, a light depression, or no mental illness at all. They are no more deserving of blame than the man at the rest stop vehemently insisting he is not a Bostonian. We can't get well until we accept that we are sick. We can't be strong, even Boston strong, until we know that we are weak.

From *New England Psychologist*, June 2013.

EIGHT

At Work in This Time and Place

As we have just seen in Chapter Seven, our lives are rooted in a particular time and place. When we talk about our work, we become even more specific. While I am an American of the twentieth and twenty-first centuries, I am also a psychologist who has spent the major part of his career working in clinics and hospitals operated by the Massachusetts Department of Mental Health from 1975 to 2015.

My forty-year career has taken me from outpatient clinics where I worked with children and families to four state-operated psychiatric hospitals built in the last three centuries. I changed jobs when the facilities where I worked were closed or turned over to private corporations in often unsuccessful attempts to save money.

The so-called savings came from the reduced salaries of mental health professionals while administrators reaped the financial rewards. The real cost was borne by the children and adults who counted on those facilities and the staff they trusted to help them through the long process of recovery from serious mental illness.

As I moved from one hospital to another, my sense of dislocation mirrored in a small way the much greater feelings of confusion and displacement that our patients experienced when they lost the people and places that, for some of them, represented their main source of security. I am not equating my inconvenience with the suffering of my patients, but sometimes even a small share in the distress of another is enough to boost our empathy by reminding us that we are not so different after all.

In a particularly unsettling time beginning in July of 1991, I changed jobs three times in a period of fourteen months, moving from an outpatient children's clinic to a locked adult unit in the same building, next to the state's only psychiatric hospital for children, and then to Westborough State Hospital, an adult facility where I spent the next eighteen years of my career.

I was on the move again in April of 2010 when the Department of Mental Health closed the hospital as part of a long-term plan to consolidate the state hospitals in Westborough and nearby Worcester into a new facility located on the Worcester grounds.

Westborough closed three years before construction of the new hospital was complete, resulting in a flurry of patient discharges to newly funded community residences, staff layoffs, and the "bumping" of staff with less seniority by those who had more. When things settled down, the remaining staff and patients relocated to Worcester State Hospital to share a single building, a 1950s-era addition to what had been the first state hospital in the country when it opened its doors in 1833.

After working in the same hospital for almost two decades, I had begun another career transition with the challenges of saying goodbye to old friends, colleagues, and patients and hello to a new work community in a new setting with unfamiliar traditions and its own distinct history. I and my Westborough colleagues were newcomers to an established family, and like newcomers everywhere, we had to learn the lore, legends, and rules of our new home. The psychologists at Worcester made us feel welcome even as they coped with the stress of departmental reorganization and changing job duties occasioned by our arrival.

While recovery from serious mental illness remained the overarching goal, we were being asked to discharge patients more quickly to community services that were not yet fully developed. At the same time, we were admitting more patients with current criminal charges and histories of dangerous behavior that required a more deliberate approach to risk assessment and reduction.

Psychologists were tapped for this function in addition to a reduced amount of our usual work providing the individual and group psychotherapy that our patients needed to recover. It was the old story of demand exceeding supply and doing our best with limited resources even as we were adjusting to the closing of one hospital and settling in to another.

After months of delay, the new Worcester Recovery Center and Hospital opened in October of 2012, and as described in the column"Moving Day for a Hospital," patients and staff made the short trip down the hill to the new facility in a single day. A patient who had gone to sleep in a room with two or, in some cases, four beds the night before would retire this night in a private room with closet space, a desk, and his own bathroom.

Worcester State Hospital, the oldest in the country, had closed its doors after 179 years, making way for the newest hospital in the land right next door.

The essays in this chapter aim to capture the experience of patients and staff living and working in hospitals built as long ago as 1833 and as recently as 2012, to describe how it feels when hospitals close, and what it's like to start again with new people in a new place, with a new mission and new hope.

To begin our journey, I invite you to join me as I climb down the old wooden stairs to the basement of a cottage at Westborough State Hospital. Stand back from the steam hissing from the old pipe in the corner while I cover the wheel with a towel and give it a turn that will give us just the right amount of heat to work comfortably today.

WESTBOROUGH STATE HOSPITAL:
THEN AND NOW

In this season of cool evenings and warm afternoons, I have become accustomed to beginning my day at the hospital by climbing down a short flight of wooden steps into the dark, concrete-floored basement of the wood-framed cottage where I work and turning down the heat. The air is thick with steam that has been sizzling overnight through miles of pipe beginning at the hospital powerhouse over the brow of a hill and across a busy road. Brushing away the occasional cobweb, I hunch over to the far corner of the basement and the valve regulating the rush of steam into the building. I cover the hissing iron wheel with a towel, and a few clockwise turns restore first the silence and then, gradually, a comfortable temperature for those who work here.

In most parts of our more than one-hundred-year-old hospital, there are easier ways to regulate the temperature. Even so, I am beginning to realize that my morning ritual connects me to the history of this place. I wonder how many more potentially useful connections remain unnoticed.

I find myself thinking about this during a recent meeting of our unit's executive committee in the hospital library. My attention is divided between the business of the day and a wall of old textbooks and hospital records that rises above us. The unit director is talking about a plan to turn three of the hospital's houses into community residences.

While the issues are being formulated and examined, my eyes drift to a row of slender, leather-bound volumes, the *Annual Reports of the State Board of Lunacy and Charity*, beginning with the year 1885. After the meeting, I resolve to come back at my first opportunity to see what was on the minds and agendas of our predecessors.

Dr. N. Emmons Paine, the first superintendent of the Westborough Insane Hospital, writes, "Although not yet completed according to the plans of the Trustees, this establishment was opened December 1, 1886 by proclamation of the Governor, and now contains more than 100 inmates."

He goes on to describe the main building with its unique architectural features. "The most marked of these is the common dining hall for about 200 patients, and the kitchen near it, at such a short distance that the meals of the patients can be served without delay, and thus brought upon the tables hotter than is usually done in our hospitals and asylums." Other smaller dining rooms serve special classes of patients on the extreme wings of the building, providing an opportunity, according to Dr. Paine, to compare the advantages of small and large dining halls.

Now, 113 years after Dr. Paine's report, we continue to look for the best ways to use architecture to promote rehabilitation. In 1992, a contingent of chronically ill patients was transferred from a locked hospital unit to three open houses. The new setting provided a more comfortable environment and the chance to develop or relearn social competency skills important for life outside the hospital.

Between 1992 and 2000, some thirty patients were discharged from the open setting, some after having spent twenty years or more in the hospital. In our open houses, patients prepare communal meals with food delivered from the hospital's main kitchen and learn to work cooperatively with one another and with staff. The hospital's original central dining hall is now used primarily for special functions. With the planned conversion of three open houses to community residences, the house originally built for Superintendent Paine is being remodeled to meet the needs of patients not yet ready for discharge.

One hundred years ago, the *Sixteenth Annual Report of the Trustees of the Westborough Insane Hospital* contained recommendations for building cottages for patients on the west side of Lake Chauncy to ease overcrowding in the main hospital buildings, to enlarge the dining room in Ward 7, to build a new ice house, and to construct a fence to keep "undesirable people" from the "pleasure grounds" on the east side of the lake off hospital property. The superintendent at the time, Dr. George Adams, also wrote, "The distribution of heat in the winter can also be greatly improved by the installation of modern appliances."

Now, a century later, I walk from the hospital's main building to my office in a cottage built by a family to provide a comfortable residence for one of their sons who was a long-term patient here. My arms are laden with modern photocopies of historical documents including the first annual report of Superintendent Paine. Paine Hall on my right is undergoing extensive renovations for its new role as a treatment center for the Department of Youth Services. Directly across from my office, the superintendent's residence is being turned into housing for our long-term patients.

Back at my desk, I scan the historical documents, pausing at the list of hospital personnel and their salaries in 1900. The superintendent and physician each earn $2,500 per year. There are assistant physicians, nurses, a baker, a meat cutter, a carpenter, farmer, and coachman. There are, of course, no psychologists in 1900, but there is something else, an occupation I had never heard of before. I notice there are two "basement boys," each earning sixteen dollars per month and then I remember it is time to turn up the heat.

From *Massachusetts Psychologist*, May 2000.

TEACHING THESE STONES TO SING: A TRIBUTE TO NORTHAMPTON STATE HOSPITAL

This is a story about teaching a hospital to sing. Next month, part two of this story will describe the concert. The stones of Northampton State Hospital didn't come into the world singing. This is how and why they were taught.

On the eighteenth of November, hundreds of speakers installed throughout the interior of Northampton State Hospital were scheduled to pour out Bach's *Magnificat* on the fields and farms and streets of the surrounding area. The project was undertaken by Anna Schuleit, an energetic visual artist and mental health advocate, determined to help this historic institution and the men and women who lived, worked, and died there to tell their stories.

Northampton State Hospital was founded in 1856, closed in 1991, and is now scheduled for demolition. Before it falls to the wrecking ball, Anna Schuleit wanted it to sing.

I first met Anna on a warm, late summer afternoon when her research into the history of our state hospitals brought her to Westborough. She had arranged a tour of the grounds with Martin Proulx, an occupational therapy assistant and staff historian and naturalist, and I eagerly accepted his invitation to tag along.

Although we had never before met Anna, there was no mistaking the identity of the tall, angular woman who strode purposefully toward us across the parking lot. She greeted us warmly, and we set out immediately on the path around the western shore of Lake Chauncy in search of the hospital's past.

With his extensive knowledge of the history of the hospital and the land, Martin was the perfect guide, and we soon found ourselves on a less traveled path on the far side of the lake. We picked our way among stones forming the foundation of what looked like a cellar that we entered by carefully descending a more recently added concrete ramp. Standing among rooms partitioned by the remnants of stone walls, we gazed into a chamber illuminated by a shaft of sunlight falling through a circular opening in the roof. The light fell on an oven in the corner. Was this a kitchen for the six cottages that once formed a colony for patients on this side of the lake, or was it the hospital crematorium?

We had all heard the stories of the forgotten dead in state hospitals, but Anna brought a new perspective. She knew what it was like to walk through an overgrown meadow on the grounds of Grafton State Hospital until the repeated rising and falling of the land underfoot told her she was walking through a graveyard.

The graves were unmarked, but Anna confirmed her suspicions by examining plot plans at the town hall. This kind of detective work is going on all over the state.

On October 22 of this year, Raja Mishra of the *Boston Globe* reported the discovery of 675 graves hidden by brambles and overgrowth on the side of a hill on the grounds of Danvers State Hospital which also closed in 1991.

The first grave on this site was found three years ago by Pat Deegan, a psychologist and former patient, who stepped on one of the small stone disks while hiking on the grounds. Deegan's discovery led to a campaign that has grown to a loose network of about two hundred people who are determined to memorialize the dead by recovering and displaying their names and preserving the cemeteries. The *Globe* article estimates that there are some ten thousand graves like this in Massachusetts.

As we moved farther along the line of foundation stones and then returned to the hospital on a path closer to the lake, we speculated about the forgotten dead of this institution. Who were they, and even now, were we walking over their bones, or had their ashes drifted away long ago? The answers to these questions are important. Each of these lives, no matter how shattered or obscure, has a dignity that deserves our attention and respect. Each has a story to tell and a lesson to teach.

As another chapter in the history of mental hospitals draws to an end with the impending demolition of Northampton State Hospital, Anna Schuleit made it possible for the stories of that institution to be told and heard. Years of tireless effort to organize a fitting tribute to the hospital culminated in a two-day open forum on November 17 and 18.

In addition to invited presentations by a panel of experts on the history and future of mental hospitals, the event included first-person accounts by former patients, photography and art exhibitions, and the playing of Bach's *Magnificat* through the empty corridors of the old hospital buildings. Anna Schuleit taught the stones of Northampton to sing, and I suspect that the music will continue to echo through the land long after the concert has ended. The least we can do is listen.

From *Massachusetts Psychologist*, December 2000.

The Day the Hospital Sang: A Tribute to Northampton State Hospital

On the eighteenth of November, right on schedule, the crumbling hulk of the once magnificent Northampton State Hospital shook the gray shrouded hilltop with J.S. Bach's *Magnificat*. The sound poured from hundreds of speakers installed throughout the 144-year-old building. Alternately triumphal and meditative, the music captured the moods of optimism and despair that are interwoven in the history of the building and of the movement to provide compassionate treatment to the mentally ill.

As if on cue, dark clouds spit a mix of rain and snow on the hospital's turrets and rooftops, the grounds grown wild with brambles and weeds, and an estimated crowd of one thousand people. Men, women, and children, alone or in family groups, marched up the hill from the adjacent grounds of Smith College, drawn to this spot by memory, curiosity, or any number of hidden reasons of the heart or mind.

The event was the culmination of years of effort by the young artist Anna Schuleit, who had been moved by this hospital on the hill and the stories it had to tell ever since she was a high school student in the area. Anna created a forum to tell the stories of the institution, the mental health movement, and especially of the people who had spent part of their lives at Northampton. Former Governor Michael Dukakis and panels of invited experts on the history and future of mental hospitals joined the voices of former patients in an open forum on November 17 and 18.

With their historical perspectives and personal accounts fresh in our minds, we walked up the hill shortly before noon. Alone with our thoughts or with friends and family, we circled the building and listened to the music. These are the words and some thoughts they inspired in this one witness.

"My soul magnifies the Lord, and my spirit rejoices in God my Savior." We all need a savior from time to time. When Dorothea Dix traveled through Massachusetts in 1841, noticing the mentally ill living on the streets, perhaps she was motivated to save her fellow citizens from hunger and neglect. Her efforts led to the building of state hospitals like Northampton in 1856, the third such institution in the Commonwealth.

When the cornerstone of Northampton was laid on July 4, 1856, there was much rejoicing and optimism. Tim Page of the *Washington Post* quotes Edward Jarvis, one of the most influential psychologists of the time, exhorting the citizens of the town and surrounding counties to "cheer, support, and strengthen" the hospital. "…We doubt not," said Jarvis, "you will do so, and then this Hospital will ever have reason to rejoice that it is placed in the midst of an enlightened and a generous community."

"Because He has regarded the lowliness of His handmaid; for, behold, henceforth all generations shall call me blessed." Is there any group more disadvantaged than the seriously and persistently mentally ill, especially when mental illness is combined with homelessness, poverty, and stigma in a society that does not understand that we are all more alike than different? At least they took down the double-sided sign on the fence between Smith College and Northampton State Hospital. On the Smith College side, the sign read: "Danger. State Hospital Patients." On the hospital side, the message was, "Danger. Smith College Students."

"Because He Who is mighty has done great things for me, and holy is

His name." We tried to do great things for those early patients of our state hospitals. We believed that cure could be realized by a restful stay in a bucolic setting where patients and staff lived together in a family atmosphere.

By 1867, Northampton's enlightened philosophy of psychoeducation was demonstrated in lectures on brain disease given by the staff to the patients. In 1900, the hospital had a bowling alley, a croquet field, football and baseball teams. Quickly the patient census came to include more and more elderly as well as younger individuals with terminal syphilis. As a result, there were fewer discharges and treatment became more custodial.

"And His mercy is from generation to generation on those who fear Him." Overcrowding became commonplace, with hardly enough room for mercy for the 2,500 souls occupying a facility built for 250. With the rise of the community mental health center movement in the 1960s, overcrowding was relieved as more and more patients were treated closer to home. But that brought problems of its own.

"He has shown might with His arm, He has scattered the proud in the conceit of their heart. He has put down the mighty from their thrones, and has exalted the lowly." It is tragic that Northampton and hospitals like it, established for the aid and comfort of people with mental illness, in many cases, contributed to their suffering.

Just listen to the stories of some former patients: the college student sent "out back" to a place of darkness and violence for discipline after coming to the aid of one of her fellow patients; the man pleading to have his twin brother released from prison where he was sent after stabbing to death a roommate who had told him that he was the devil and would get him; the woman raped by a staff member who later died of AIDS.

We cannot listen to these stories of the "lowly" without wondering how we have participated, even in small or unknowing ways, in the work of the proud and mighty. Their stories humble and chasten us.

"He has filled the hungry with good things, and the rich He has sent away empty. He has given help to Israel, His servant, mindful of His mercy. Even as He spoke to our fathers, to Abraham and to his posterity forever."

Sometimes, the stories of former patients at Northampton and elsewhere give us cause for hope. Over and over, we hear how much the small "human" moments between patients and staff contribute to their well-being, how important it is to bring a sense of humor to work, to listen and to take seriously what the people in our hospitals have to say.

The historical perspective on treating people with mental illness brings into focus just how complex and challenging this enterprise really is. Anna Schuleit's memoriam to Northampton State Hospital reminds us of the words of the Talmud, quoted at the forum by Assistant Commissioner of Mental Health, Dr. Kenneth Duckworth: "You are not permitted to complete the task, nor should you be allowed to put it down."

From *Massachusetts Psychologist*, January 2001.

• • •

SAYING IT WITH FLOWERS

After ninety-one years of service to the citizens of Massachusetts, the Boston Psychopathic Hospital, known in modern times as the Massachusetts Mental Health Center, closed its doors this past November.

Thanks to Anna Schuleit, an installation artist and mental health advocate, the event was marked by a sea of flowers, bathing the halls, waiting rooms, and offices of this pioneering experiment in community mental health.

Ms. Schuleit first made her mark on the consciousness of the mental health community in November of 2001 with her installation to commemorate Northampton State Hospital, at the time being considered for demolition after its closing several years earlier. After a one-day academic symposium at neighboring Smith College, the shell of the empty hospital building resounded with the strains of Bach's *Magnificat* channeled through more than one hundred speakers put in place through the artist's vision.

Now it was Mass Mental's turn, and this venerable institution would not be outdone. True to her style, Ms. Schuleit appealed to the senses, this time with an explosion of bright colors and sweet smells counterpoised to the dank air and fickle light, here straining and there bursting into the empty building. All the while, concealed speakers broadcast snatches of muted conversations, part of the ambient sounds of the building recorded in the weeks before it closed.

From the moment I learned of the event, I wanted to be there. I should have had plenty of time to prepare, but the combination of a misplaced invitation and a lucky glance at the Sunday paper had me out the door before I knew what to expect.

I was drawn to the old building on Fenwood Road because I was a psychologist working in the state hospital system and because, after attending the Northampton event, I knew I would be moved, and I hoped to be surprised. But there was something else pulling me to Boston that morning, maybe the most important thing of all. Thirty-one years earlier, I had completed my internship at Mass

Mental. And so, at a moment's notice, I got in the car that bright Sunday morning in November and headed for the city, prepared for nothing in particular and counting on the unexpected.

In the three decades since completing my internship at Mass Mental, I have cherished memories and enjoyed reunions, official and otherwise, with my former colleagues and supervisors. Still, I have only been back to the building on a few occasions, most recently more than twenty years ago.

The old neighborhood has seen a great deal of change in the last two decades. The center itself, a massive brick structure, still seems as out of place as ever on its street of large, wood-framed, multi-family houses. But now this old hulk of a building and its working-class neighbors have company. The sleek form of a high-tech medical tower soars over the roofs across the street, and a sprawl of suburban style condominiums fans out from the hospital's back door. Between both of these new features, the abandoned Mass Mental opened its doors for one last goodbye.

The main entrance leads to a lobby that is dark and chilly despite the brightness of the day. Visitors are invited to follow the arrows taped to the wall and wander the corridors and courtyards, guided only by the thoughts that come with the stirring of all the senses. Sight, sound, smell, and the damp feel of the air in this indoor garden evoke a welter of conflicting impressions that drive me to the solitude of an old picnic table to collect my thoughts. I am not there long before one of the event's volunteer crew approaches and introduces himself as a consumer of mental health services from another part of the country here to help memorialize the Mass Mental Health Center.

When I told him that I had once been an intern here, he began asking questions about the hospital as well as about the broader scope of inpatient mental health services in Massachusetts. I told him what I could and listened longer than I intended to his impassioned arguments for the preservation of asylums. As this one closed, he looked around at the flowers and saw what he could describe only as a funeral.

By filling the hospital with flowers, the artist said she was attempting to deliver some of the long-overdue bouquets that we never think to bring to loved ones hospitalized for the treatment of mental illness. For too many years, the stigma associated with psychiatric problems has made it easier to leave our flowers at home. That day last November, however, Anna Schuleit tried to right one of the many wrongs born of centuries of ostracizing the mentally ill. She supplied the flowers and left the rest up to us.

I had come here to discover the part that was up to me. Looking for the unexpected, I was not disappointed to find that the flowers evoked neither the sadness of death nor the hope of restitution. It was something more like the continuity of a garden. I had come to say goodbye to an empty, lifeless building, and I wound up spending most of my time listening to a stranger's story. Isn't that what I had learned to do in this very building so many years ago? Isn't that what I still carry with me from my year at Mass Mental?

While the realist in me rejects the tidy ending, things are what they are. The day after the installation closed, the artist, true to her word, distributed the flowers to the few mental hospitals still open in Massachusetts. When I saw the African violets on the conference table at morning rounds, I knew I had found what I was looking for.

From *Massachusetts Psychologist*, January 2004.

THE LUCKIEST MAN IN THE WORLD

I just met the luckiest man in the world, or at least, that's what he told me. It turns out I have known him for many years, but like so much that we are learning about one another in the last days of the hospital, his disclosure came as a surprise. You would not think that a person who has suffered from a particularly virulent form of schizophrenia for more than thirty years could consider himself lucky. That kind of self-assessment would surely be the mark of delusional thinking that would seal the diagnosis, if there were ever any doubt in the first place. There never was.

The luckiest man in the world is a pleasant fellow, although I have heard that he has not always been so. We first met when I interviewed him seventeen years ago for an annual progress review and his rapidly shifting focus of attention and discourse made it clear that my work in an outpatient child and family program was indeed over. This was the state hospital, and the fellow in the chair on the other side of my desk was introducing me to my new professional home.

I didn't know he was the luckiest man in the world, but I sensed both his intellectual curiosity and his optimism when he asked me if it was true that there were positive symptoms of schizophrenia. He reasoned that a condition that had caused so much disruption in his life must have some redeeming qualities. If only it did. In the months and years that followed, I would see this fellow in passing, have him as a member of a creative writing group and an emotion management group, and serve as the psychologist on his treatment team.

I learned about his early successes and how close he had come to graduating from college, trying again and again to complete his studies even after he started to develop symptoms.

The voices were the worst. Even when they were benign, their constant chatter made it hard to concentrate on anything else. When they were harsh and critical, he took their reproaches to heart. And so, the luckiest man in the world started wearing headphones, filling his head with his favorite music to drive out the soul-killing noise that shattered his peace of mind. He enjoyed the music and the lucid conversations he would have with anyone interested in talking about the rock bands of the sixties.

The luckiest man in the world loved a good story and he liked to write. He gave it his best effort in a creative writing group, but at first, all he could do was take dictation from the voices that had hijacked his thought processes. In time, he learned to segregate his thoughts from the message of the voices, separating one from the other with a bold line slashed across the page. On his best days, he could resist the verbatim dictation and incorporate the gist of the message into a coherent narrative.

Perhaps you can understand my surprise when this fellow began a recent group session by saying he is the luckiest man in the world. As always, we waited to see if he was beginning to express a straightforward, logically constructed message or if a grandiose delusional assessment of himself would trail off into unrelated fragments of thought.

He said that he knows he has a mental illness, which he certainly never wanted. Nevertheless, he also knows he is getting the care he needs in the hospital from staff he respects, trusts, and likes. The grounds are beautiful, the sun is shining, and he is sitting in a room with people willing to listen to what he has to say. The luckiest man in the world went on to say that he knows the hospital is closing, that he is not sure where he will go, but that somehow, he will wind up where he is supposed to be. He also said that he does not always believe any of this, but he does today, and that is good enough for now.

What are we to make of the luckiest man in the world? His self-as-sessment is certainly delusional, clearly exaggerated, but unquestionably true. Philosophers through the ages have grappled with the very issues he boldly addresses: the mystery of individual existence in one set of circumstances and not another, the process of recognizing and accepting those circumstances, the challenge of finding a calling in our own version of life's struggles, and the discovery of a completely unjustified hope in an unknown future.

As young children we realize that we are different from everyone else and later, that we are stuck with being who we are. As time goes on, we may come to see that who we are isn't so bad after all. Finally, if we are lucky, we may conclude that our particular life was the best one we could have had. Our best thinkers and writers have expressed all of these ideas with more thought and grace but, in my experience, none more simply, honestly, or memorably than the luckiest man in the world.

From *New England Psychologist*, January 2010.

• • •

THE BIRTH OF A NEW HOSPITAL

In the course of my career as a psychologist, I have witnessed the closing of many of the hospitals where I have worked, but I have never seen a new one open. That is about to change with the scheduled opening of the new Worcester Recovery Center and Hospital in July of 2012. Every day is a step closer to the awakening of the sleeping giant that shares a hilltop with the last functioning building of Worcester State Hospital, a 1950s-era, eight-story afterthought to the original 1876 structure destroyed in a 1991 fire. All that remains of the original hospital are the shell of an administration building, a turret, and the hospital's iconic clock tower. Beside these elegant remains of the past, the new structure is stirring, breathing with exhalations of gray smoke from a modern heating system, and keeping watch through windows illuminated late into each passing night.

I have had the opportunity to work in city and, by the standards of their time, rural hospitals built in three different centuries and designed according to the principles of prevailing ideas about the nature of illness and recovery.

Cottage plan hospitals gave me the opportunity to do psychotherapy on long walks with patients through the open countryside. The design gained popularity at the very end of the nineteenth century and continued to be very popular well into the twentieth. These hospitals are distinguished by a collection of small buildings, usually of no more than two stories, spread across large tracts of open land, far enough away from the stresses of city life to provide a restful, healing environment.

The cottage plan was inspired by the village of Gheel in Belgium where families traditionally opened their homes to neighbors with mental illness who became part of the household, sharing in the work and daily life of their hosts.

In my own experience, this aspect of the cottage plan came to life in the emphasis these institutions placed on rehabilitation and the learning or relearning of social and practical skills of daily living. Communal living in small houses gave patients the opportunity to work together with staff to plan and prepare meals, do necessary household chores, and make excursions into the community that eased their transitions to life after discharge.

The antithesis of the cottage plan was the urban hospital where I did my predoctoral internship. From its founding in the early 1900s, this institution partnered with a university teaching and research center to promote the discovery of new knowledge and more effective treatment. Its philosophy of recovery also emphasized the advantages that patients enjoyed by remaining close to their families and not shunted aside to remote country locations where they risked being forgotten and further alienated from the world.

Kirkbride hospitals, whose name derives from the plan developed by psychiatrist Thomas Story Kirkbride in the middle part of the nineteenth century, in many ways combine the best features of cottage and urban institutions.

They are typically situated in areas of natural beauty with extensive grounds affording opportunities for rest, recreation, and productive activity. Unlike cottage plan hospitals, however, Kirkbride institutions are dominated by a massive building with a central administration area and two wings, segregated by sex, diagnosis, and acuity of symptoms. Every section of every wing affords its residents access to fresh air and clear views of the surrounding countryside. At the same time, higher functioning patients are protected from what was thought to be the negative influence of less stable individuals by the separation of patients according to their emotional and behavioral stability.

The new Worcester Recovery Center and Hospital occupies the site where the original Kirkbride building of Worcester State Hospital once stood. A graceful arc of three to four stories, it faces the clock tower in a symbolic expression of the new embracing the old. The building incorporates the latest thinking in hospital design as does every new hospital in every age. The new building maximizes natural light and views of the surrounding landscape. It minimizes noise with special carpet tiles and incorporates the ideal blend of privacy and communal living with residential units conceptualized as houses and clusters of units sharing the common space of neighborhoods. All of the neighborhoods look out onto a central atrium or downtown area containing some of the essential services and amenities of any community: a bank, convenience store, library, and access to an outdoor village green.

The building will be ready for occupancy in July. Every day it begins to feel more like a living presence, its breath visible in plumes of smoke, its groans heard in the whirr of unnamed machinery. There is even a kind of intelligence that gleams in the evening lights from its windows. As for its soul, the lives that will be played out and the stories told within its walls—that is for us to begin to provide.

From *New England Psychologist*, March 2012.

• • •

MOVING DAY FOR A HOSPITAL

On the first Tuesday in October 2012, 130 people being treated for mental illness quietly slipped away from Worcester State Hospital. They were preceded by more than three times that number of staff who had started the exodus the previous week.

The first group boarded a luxury motor coach at eight in the morning for the quarter-mile ride to the new Worcester Recovery Center and Hospital just down the hill from the 1950s-era building that was the last remnant of one of the first state hospitals in the country. The move was the culmination of nearly a decade of planning and construction of a new facility designed to help people learn to manage their mental illnesses so they might return to the community to pursue their hopes and dreams.

When I wrote about this project six months ago, the nearly completed building seemed to be lacking only the people whose stories would be told and reworked within its walls. Now we are here, and this is how it happened.

The new hospital was originally scheduled to open on August 21, but as is the case with most new construction, hidden surprises that need to be addressed come to light as the work proceeds. We knew that something would have to be done about the nearly two-hundred-year-old clock tower from the original hospital, a symbol of the old embraced by the new, that was structurally too unstable to leave in place.

The tower was to be taken down and replaced by a smaller version composed of old and new building materials. Did the demolition have to be complete before the new hospital opened, or could it be done later? If it had to be done first, then why was the tower still standing?

There was no shortage of rumors to explain the delay. One involved the historical society's determination to document the location of every brick in the existing structure presumably to guide those charged with reconstructing a mini-tower with some of these same materials.

As rumors go, my personal favorite had it that a protected species of bird was nesting in the old tower and would have to be relocated before demolition could begin. Of course, there were more mundane and probably more accurate theories about why the building was not ready for occupancy in August. You don't take possession of a $500 million building unless you are as certain as you can be that there are no major construction flaws.

For most of us, it mattered little whether we moved into the new hospital in August or at some later date. We continued to tour the facility and became more familiar with its sprawling layout on every visit. We described the building to our patients and explained how it would promote a recovery model of treatment. We had time to pack and to discard the accretions of years so that we could travel light into our new workplace. As psychologists, there is really very little we need to do our work. For better or worse, we are the instruments of the changes our patients want to make in their lives. All we really need is what we have learned about human behavior and the capacity to listen reflectively and respond with empathy, curiosity, and good sense.

It is no small task to move a hospital, to bring people, apparatus, equipment, medical records, and supplies to a designated place at an appointed time in the right sequence without loss or damage. While our administrators managed the logistics of the move, we were free to address the human dimension.

We learned that we could not generalize about how people would respond to the move. To assume that everyone would be pleased to trade a run-down hospital building for a shiny new structure with all the conveniences that modern technology could provide is to miss the incontrovertible fact that the only place most people wanted to move to was home.

When the day came, the actual move took no more than a few hours. Because the existing hospital units were reorganized, there were new groupings of patients and staff facing the challenge of working together in a new environment. For some, the situation was the quintessential fresh start. For others, the change evoked anxiety that their privileges would be decreased and their momentum toward discharge slowed as their new clinical teams took time to get to know them.

In those first days, the staff gave reassurance, dispensed information, confessed ignorance, and promised to do our best to find out what we didn't know and address the glitches that appear in the best made plans and the best made buildings. We toured the building together, got lost together, laughed, showed patience with one another, and began to appreciate all the comforts, conveniences, and opportunities of this beautiful new place. The builders had done their work well, and now we were making a good start on ours.

From *New England Psychologist*, November 2012.

NINE

Keeping the Flame Alive

One of the most satisfying aspects of my career as a clinical psychologist has been the opportunity to teach and supervise graduate students during their practicum and internship years at the clinics and hospitals where I worked.

In my first job after postdoctoral training, I started by supervising students in weekly individual meetings. There, we discussed the student's work with each of his or her patients, issues of teamwork, agency policies, the larger social, economic, and political context in which we worked, and how all of this related to the theories and practices of clinical psychology that they were learning in graduate school. We also got to know one another, sharing stories about our own education and life experiences that informed the way we understood people.

When I started in 1975, there were no formal courses in how to conduct clinical supervision. Like most of my colleagues, I used my own experience with supervisors as a guide. I knew what was helpful and what was not, and I tried to emulate my very best teachers. What all of these men and women had in common was an easy manner and a sense of being approachable. They communicated a genuine interest in me and in my development as a psychologist. They were reassuring, encouraging, generous in answering questions and sharing information, humble in acknowledging ignorance, and resourceful in helping me to find the answers I needed.

They made me think about people and their challenges in new ways so that I often came away from our meetings feeling more hopeful and less stuck in my work. Thinking differently about situations is a key factor in coping with the challenges in our own lives and in helping our patients do the same. My best supervisors taught me this practice.

Starting as an individual supervisor, I quickly assumed the duties of recruiting, interviewing, and selecting students for practicum placements. For the reader who is not familiar with the education and training of a doctoral level clinical psychologist, let me explain that in a typical four-year doctoral program, students spend the first three years supplementing their classroom instruction with part-time clinical work in a clinic or hospital under the supervision of one or more of the agency's licensed clinical psychologists. This practice is referred to as practicum training.

The fourth year of the doctoral program is devoted to a full-time internship consisting of an organized program of clinical practice, supervision, and weekly lectures on topics relevant to the students' work and professional development. The most rigorous internships are accredited by the American Psychological Association, and competition for these positions is intense. Every year there are more applicants than there are available slots, and some students are forced to re-apply the next year or to accept an internship not accredited by the APA.

In addition to classroom instruction and clinical training, doctoral candidates are expected to write a dissertation based on original research for Ph.D. programs or on a literature review or demonstration project for Doctor of Psychology (Psy.D.) programs.

After three years of attending to the details of recruiting, selecting, and supervising practicum students in my first job, I accepted a position as the Director of Psychology Training in the Children's Outpatient Department at the Boston University Medical Center in 1978.

For the next thirty-seven years in three different hospitals, I would continue to serve as a director or co-director of practicum or APA-accredited internship programs. I gladly took on the responsibilities of these positions in addition to my usual duties as a staff psychologist because they provided opportunities to teach and mentor bright and compassionate men and women dedicated to improving the lives of others.

In all of the hospitals where I worked, my fellow supervisors shared my enthusiasm for the task. With common ideals and values about the power of psychology to help people lead healthier, more satisfying lives, staff and students worked together to help the people we served meet the challenges they faced.

Whatever I may have taught my students about the theory and practice of clinical psychology, I know I have learned from them as well. They have shared information from the classroom and tested it against the real world of patient care, and in the process, there were many times when we both learned something new.

They have shared their interests and life experiences as we discussed their hopes and plans for their professional careers. In the exchange, I have offered stories of how my own combination of choice and chance brought me to this time and place and the conversation taking place between us.

You cannot do this work in an impersonal way. Clinical psychology is a profession where the practitioner is the instrument of the change the client is trying to make. When you sit face-to-face with someone in the consulting room, you bring your knowledge, experience, judgment, empathy, compassion, and unwavering attention.

You monitor your own emotions, deciding which, if any, to share with your client and which simply to observe as a clue to what is happening between you. When you teach someone to become a clinical psychologist, you enter this emotional realm in a way that allows you to get to know one another. Good supervisors care about their students. And because we cared, we did everything we could to maintain the integrity of our training programs when budget cuts, supervisor layoffs, the shutdown of units, and in 2010, the abrupt closing of Westborough State Hospital threatened the very existence of the training enterprise.

Whatever else was going on around us in the larger organization, we continued to provide the security of a regular routine for our students with patient-care responsibilities, supervision sessions, and weekly seminars.

When Westborough State Hospital closed in April of 2010, three months before the end of the internship year, we moved the program to Worcester State Hospital so our students could complete their training. Our colleagues at Worcester, who were operating their own internship, graciously made room for us to continue the work we had begun.

After five hospitals, scores of colleagues, and hundreds of patients and students, I retired from my position as a psychologist with the Massachusetts Department of Mental Health in June of 2015.

I made the decision to leave over a period of many months with all of the ambivalence and uncertainty that might be expected after a long career doing mostly what I loved. Once I made my decision, I felt a sense of urgency to share all that I knew about clinical psychology with my students as if I were passing a torch that I had been carrying since the beginning of my career. I had done my part, and now it was up to the new generation to keep the flame alive.

Yet the metaphor fails because mine is not the only torch that my students will carry. As one of my patients said long ago, we are each "the product of many people." We bring our own light into the world, but the spark is kindled by the lights of those who have gone before us and ignites a flame in those who follow.

OF CONTRACTS AND COVENANTS

My briefcase is always heavier than it needs to be, heavy with work that I know I'll never touch but bring home anyway, and heavy with things that are just too important not to have by my side. Tonight, at the beginning of October, I am carrying five blank contracts to be distributed in the morning to the supervisors of our psychology trainees.

These are the typical documents spelling out the mutual obligations of the training institution and its students—hours to be worked, compensation to be paid, kinds of psychological services to be rendered, and the amount and type of supervision to be provided. Contracts such as these have become more fashionable since my own days as a graduate student and are now required by most schools and training sites. This emphasis on explicit contractual relationships is not unique to the training of psychologists and other mental health professionals but has come to permeate a broad range of interpersonal transactions from the business world to our personal lives.

The new training contracts share the dark recesses of my briefcase with other pieces of paper that bear the evidence of a different kind of work relationship. There is a paper written for class by a former intern in which he demonstrates the terrible synergy between his patient's history of loss, the closing of one of our hospital's units, and a devastating personal loss in his own life.

It lies next to the contributions of a colleague and a student—two cartoons lampooning, in one case, the smugness of dogmatic psychological theory and, in another, changes in psychotherapy under managed care. From a patient, there is a poem, "Mental illness is a drag/To keep hammering at the walls impassive,/Until passively I surrender."

And there is the farewell address of the director of the now closed Gaebler Children's Center, commenting on the "universal fellowship of those who work with the most difficult children" that "has always been intensely felt at Gaebler."

These more personal expressions of sadness, joy, frustration, and comradeship are not the stuff of contracts but the evidence of what Max DePree in his book *Leadership is An Art* calls covenants. While contracts define the letter of the law, covenants convey its spirit. Contracts may be necessary to clarify the mutual obligations of parties in a relationship, but they are never sufficient to ensure the well-being of true partners. A contract may launch an enterprise, but only a covenant can guarantee that it will survive change, conflict, and the challenge of helping individuals achieve their full potential.

DePree points out that covenantal relationships are not mere frills or luxuries in the life of an institution but ingredients necessary to an institution's survival. A business, a university, a department of psychology, a hospital cannot thrive unless it nurtures and serves both its clients and employees.

It is a sad paradox of our times that now, when the forces of social isolation and a dissolving sense of community make covenants between people more important than ever, they are becoming harder to find.

Writing in the September 1995 issue of the *APA Monitor*, Tori DeAngelis cited the increased pace of technology, industrialization, and social mobility as major forces contributing to growing feelings of isolation and loneliness among an increasingly larger segment of our population.

At the same time, there is abundant evidence that the potential of the workplace to bring people together through their commitment to shared values is being eroded by a widespread neglect of employees' rights and corporate policies that border on or, in some cases, cross the line to frank exploitation. In the worst situations, it makes little sense to talk about missing opportunities to build covenants when obligations to honor contracts are ignored.

Developing covenants is a nice example of an institution's ability to do well by doing good. DePree's own company, Herman Miller, Inc., a North Carolina furniture manufacturer, was named one of the most profitable in America and one of the best companies to work for in terms of wages and working conditions. DePree would be the first to say that earning both of these distinctions is no coincidence, and I'm sure that most of us can find evidence for a similar link between nurture and productivity in our own experience.

Tomorrow when I distribute the training contracts to the supervisors of our students, I will do so as an act of faith and an act of hope. There is faith in the professionalism and sensitivity of the trusted colleagues with whom I share this work as well as in the openness and sincerity of our new trainees. There is hope that our work together can withstand the accelerated pace of change that makes it difficult to predict the challenges we will face in the coming year.

Finally, there is the hope that by some modern-day alchemy, five blank contracts jammed into a briefcase in the fall will be replaced next summer by a few scraps of paper written in the language of covenants.

From *Massachusetts Psychologist*, October 1995.

• • •

SIGNS OF THE TIMES

June is the time of endings and beginnings, graduations or, to use the more forward-looking term, commencements. At Westborough State

Hospital, or wherever psychology students do their clinical training, June is the time to say goodbye and good luck. The message that I send to our own departing interns is one which I hope my colleagues involved in supervision and teaching will also find relevant for their students. In the tradition of my father, who painted messages on road signs, I turn to signs for the words to express my own thoughts and feelings about the training year.

Two messages come to mind, separated by the width of our country. One is a recorded announcement familiar to anyone who has visited Florida's Disney World, and the other, a small sign visible from the ski lift at Sugarloaf Mountain in Maine.

At the end of a typical ride at Disney World, a recorded voice announces, "This concludes our visit to the World of Imagination. Please check your seats for your belongings, take small children by the hand, and exit the vehicle. Please step onto the platform, which is moving at the same speed as your vehicle, and exit to the right."

After ten months of clinical training, your visit to this psychiatric World of Imagination has come to an end. Whatever you thought about these brick walls and the people inside when you arrived in September, now your own experience will inform your judgment. As with most visitors to this strange culture, your time here has probably made its inhabitants seem less strange, more human, more like yourselves. In the brief course of your training with us, you have explored the intricacies of the World of Imagination. You have seen the face of imagination gone awry in the eyes of the woman who told you time and again of her paralyzing fear that she will be abducted and killed by the Mafia, Satanists, or an old boss that she cannot stop thinking about. You have wished with all your heart that your own imagination would supply you with just the right words to exorcise the demons that torture her.

Do check your seats for your belongings. It would be a pity to leave behind the important things that you brought with you in September. Your warmth, sensitivity, passion to understand, and the energy and enthusiasm that keep you going—these are the gifts we invited you here to develop and share. Make sure you have them all on the way out.

Other things you may wish to throw away, like your belief that therapists must be all-knowing, all-powerful, and forever kind. If you haven't already discarded these items, receptacles are provided by the exits.

Take small children by the hand. They are still too little and too frail to thrive without being carefully tended. So are the new insights that you have gained during this training year. You have marveled at the schizophrenic man who speaks in word salad but can still summon the angels when he raises his fiddle to heaven and begins to play. You have learned that a patient's deepest secrets shared with you in the sanctity of a therapy session are but fragments of a puzzle that takes an entire team to solve. Everywhere you look, you have seen sadness, depression, grief, and you have begun to wonder if this is the mental illness or the reaction to what the illness has robbed.

Step carefully now onto the platform. Do not be concerned that your vehicle will not stop. Remember, the platform is also moving—just as fast, maybe faster. A ride through a psychiatric hospital is never slow and leisurely, but this year, the pace has been especially brisk. In the best of times, you are riding through a fun house where the tracks swerve unexpectedly in the dark and you are scared witless by challenges springing from the walls. This year, the walls themselves have shifted as you passed, dropping great chunks of concrete around you and opening gaping cracks in the floor.

You have endured the reorganization of the hospital, the loss of supervisors through layoffs and transfers, and the challenge of helping your patients adapt to change even as you had to face again reminders of personal changes that you would have rather forgotten. We neither planned nor could have predicted the upheavals that took place during your year with us, but we hope the experience has made you stronger. It was a fast and wild ride, and it continues everywhere outside the walls of this hospital.

There is one more sign to describe, and it needs no explanation. My daughter spotted it from the ski lift at Sugarloaf. The message, clear and simple, is our heartfelt parting word to you all. "We care about you. Expect the unexpected."

From *Massachusetts Psychologist*, June 1995.

• • •

PARADE OF STARS

The arrival of our new psychology interns at the hospital in September is surely as much a sign of fall as the first hints of color in the New England foliage. Their appearance is the culmination of a year-long process of updating our program brochures and online descriptions, reading scores of applications, interviewing our top candidates, and biting our nails through the mutual selection process that somehow delivers these fledging psychologists to our doorstep. The sudden-ness of their appearance suggests there is magic at work, but the work is really done by our directors of training, psychologists from our hospital and affiliated sites, and administrative assistants who make the phone calls, type the schedules, and arrange the space for the orientation sessions, welcoming talks, and something called the Parade of Stars.

I have been participating in this parade since I arrived here nearly five years ago, but only recently did I ask how the event got its name. Not sure was the most frequent response. We've always just called it that. The event itself is a series of talks that the leaders of different elective rotations present to the interns, describing the content, requirements, and opportunities of the clinical experience.

Our hospital offers six different rotations, and affiliated sites account for at least that number. With so many opportunities from which to choose, we wonder how the interns can possibly decide which four will give them the best preparation for the careers they are beginning to build. We wonder and we work hard to come up with the best sales pitch we can.

Sitting around the conference table at the Parade of Stars, we listen to our colleagues describe their rotations and watch the faces of the interns we are trying to recruit for our own. Yes, make no mistake about it, we are there on a mission. Join the Navy and see the world. Like the Marines, we're looking for a few good men and women. This process is a contest where we do our best to describe how we can provide the interns with a learning experience that is unique, interesting, and designed to teach them clinical skills that are evidence-based, valuable to society, and marketable.

We want these young people working with us because we believe the work we do and the training we provide offer something special. We want them working with us because we know how much they can already contribute to the mission of our service. They wouldn't be here if they didn't have what it takes to shine.

It is interesting to hear what my colleagues highlight when they describe the rotations they lead. Some start with a history of their program and the services they provide to the institution and its patients. We hear why these services are important and the results of research showing that they are effective.

There are accounts of how the hospital managed before these programs were implemented and how much better it functions now. The interns listen attentively. A smile here, a nod there, and the occasional scribble of notes all signal different levels of interest and attraction to the experience being described.

Another colleague takes the floor with a different approach, telling about his own time as an intern in a similar setting many years ago and how the experience pulled him in and shaped his entire career.

When my turn comes to talk about my specialty of helping people avoid dangerous behavior, I find that my colleagues have set the table for me to provide a feast of information about various kinds of risk assessments and the growing importance of this work for psychologists and society. I am not prepared for this banquet. I have come with simpler fare, and as the interns do their best to remain attentive after more than an hour of presentations, I begin with a story. In a hospital like ours, there are so many stories, but I select one about one of our patients and the creative way a previous intern helped her accept the reality of her mental illness and return to her life as a student, mother, and aspiring professional.

The story offers opportunities to explore many of the more specialized areas and techniques that form the basis of whole rotations. It is a story of how to manage mental illness, prevent relapse, think differently about life, minimize risks, and pursue recovery. It is a story I hope some of the interns can see themselves fitting into with other people who come to us when mental illness threatens to rewrite the scripts of their lives.

Unless I am imagining things, there were the usual smiles, nods, and scribbling of notes from the interns. With luck one or more of them will join me in my work, but no matter what the outcome, the Parade of Stars is a contest everyone wins.

The interns win because with so many good opportunities and the guidance of our training director, they cannot help but make wise choices. Our patients win because no matter what rotations the interns choose, our patients get the benefit of their knowledge, energy, and enthusiasm. And, as for the recruiting war among us psychologists, it reminds us how lucky we are to be part of a strong team. I've given up looking for the parade but the stars—they're everywhere.

Adapted from *New England Psychologist*, October 2014.

TEN

LIVING WITH UNCERTAINTY

The four columns in this chapter could have easily been twice that number or even more because the theme and challenge of living with uncertainty has been a part of my life for as long as I can remember. It courses through all that I have experienced and written about in the more than two decades of my "In Person" column, and while we all deal with uncertainly in different ways, I am convinced that it is one of those universals that are part of the fabric of every human life.

By the time I wrote the first of these essays, "Celebrating Life on the Edge," in July of 2006, I had been writing my column for thirteen years and living for almost sixty. In all that time, I had become accustomed to living on the edge. As the son of a blue-collar worker in a white-collar professional world, I lived on the edge of experiential know-how and specialized academic knowledge.

As an observant Catholic and a psychologist schooled in Freudian theory, my edge was the boundary between two antithetical and often competing orthodoxies. It took a wise therapist, who was both a Jesuit Catholic priest and a Freudian analyst, to tell me that he didn't like my God. "Isn't he your God too?" I wondered but was probably too timid to ask.

In time, I learned that there is a sense in which we create the God who created us by the way we think about Him or Her. Experiences of loss and failure, my own and those of others, helped me to choose a God of compassion and mercy and to find a place for Him in my faith and practice. The edge of religion and psychology was a good place to discover and live the lessons of both.

Living on the edge may be rewarding, but it isn't easy. Like a climber on a mountain ridge, the edge-dweller gets the full force of the winds from both directions and longs to plant both feet firmly on one side or the other. The comfort of being firmly rooted in orthodoxy can be seductive, but it is not without its own dangers, the twin perils of an all-or-nothing worldview and the accompanying delusion that we can guarantee success and avoid misfortune if we simply do everything the right way.

When we hunker down on one side of the ridge or the other, the shelter we find often comes at the expense of missed opportunities for learning new and deeper truths.

To live on the edge is to live with uncertainty, and this has never been easy for me. Maybe that is why, at the beginning of my career, I dreamed about finding the crystal of wisdom, a potent talisman that would always tell me exactly what I needed to say in order to be most helpful to the people who came to my office for help.

In the column "What I Didn't Get for the Holidays," I disclosed that, nearly forty years later, I am still looking for the magic crystal. With the passage of time, however, I have learned to look in different places for something that I now believe will look nothing like the original object of my search.

When you give up orthodoxy, live on the edge, and feel the stinging winds of uncertainty, you know that you are moving through a process of work and life that you cannot fully control. You set goals, make plans, prepare to act, and do your best, trying always to stay flexible, resilient, and open to the lessons of unexpected developments.

Hoping for the best but apprehensive about my future, I wrote "Learning to Trust the Process" four months before retiring from my full-time position of thirty-nine years as a psychologist with the Massachusetts Department of Mental Health. I was trying to put into writing some of the things I had learned along the way and, I suppose, to reassure myself that I was making the right decision.

Since that forking of the road, I have been traveling on new paths through old, familiar terrain. Still thinking like a psychologist, I find myself contemplating many of the same questions as I follow new routines governed more by my interests than my obligations. I am writing more, doing some clinical work, and giving the occasional lecture to clinical psychology interns at the Worcester Recovery Center and Hospital.

With more time for family and travel, my wife and I have been taking advantage of this freedom that retirement brings, limited as freedom always is by responsibilities to others.

It has been said that the developmental task of our senior years is a summing up of our lives even as we continue to live them. In childhood, we were actors, living and narrating our days by a sequence of actions. What we did was all that mattered, defining who we were even before that question had any meaning. Somewhere in adolescence, we became agents, ordering our lives toward the achievement of goals. We chose our schools for what we wanted to learn to prepare us for careers that suited our interests and abilities.

We enlarged our families as we accepted others into our hearts and lives—friends, spouses, partners, children, the young and the old—embedding ourselves in large and small communities where we could give and receive love, support, and wisdom. Now, in the summing up of all that has gone before, we can begin to see ourselves as the authors of our lives, striving to understand the reasons for our decisions, choices, successes, and failures and appreciating the consequences of our actions.

As authors, we might like to think that our choices have been rational and reasonable and that we have lived our lives just as we wanted to, but we know it isn't so. Our lives have been a product of choice and chance, edited by fortune, destiny, divine providence, or whatever name we give to the mysteries that change the script we intended to write for ourselves. This is the process that we all live and learning to trust it is the work of a lifetime.

CELEBRATING LIFE ON THE EDGE

The young man was tall and lean with the dark stubble of an accidental beard and short hair spiked from sleeping rough on the streets. He had a sinewy strength that could have belonged to an athlete fallen on hard times, but a faraway look in his eyes betrayed something more pernicious. He had left a bundle of troubles in the heartland and hitchhiked east until he reached Massachusetts where an arrest for trespassing eventually brought him to the hospital. When we asked why he had stopped here, he replied simply that he had run out of land. If he expected to find comfort in putting as much distance as possible between himself and his troubled circumstances, he might have headed north to the Canadian hinterland, but instead he came to the ocean. Perhaps there is something healing or at least distracting about fleeing to the edge of the continent, something that sustains the illusion that hard times are behind you and the future is as limitless as the horizon.

Now, in the heart of summer, we all seek our version of the geographic cure, a change of scene that takes us from lives that can become so embedded in routine that we have to remind ourselves that ours is not the only perspective on the world. Flatlanders head for the mountains, and mountain dwellers go down to the sea. Even busmen reluctant to give up the wheel steer for new destinations. We are drawn not only to something different but also to something that marks the boundary between ordinary life and its alternatives. In summer we celebrate life on the edge.

What is it about the boundaries of things that fascinates us so much? Watch children playing at the beach, and eventually you will notice one of them racing with the surf. A boy dashes across wet sand to the leading edge of an advancing wave, then turns and runs back to safety before the water touches him. As his confidence grows, he moves closer to the surf before retreating. Sooner or later the boy miscalculates and the wave catches him. He shouts with glee, keeps running, or falls on the sand in mock defeat. He has lost a round in a battle with a force of unimaginable power, but he lives to play another, and another, and another, until something more interesting captures his attention.

The game demonstrates that one of the joys of playing on the boundary of land and sea is the sense of mastery that comes from winning a contest with something so much bigger and more powerful than ourselves. Children stack the odds in their favor by making rules for the game that guarantee their safety, win or lose.

In the real world, nature plays by her own rules, and if there is any safety at all, it comes only with knowledge, experience, preparation, and sound judgment. Even so, sailors sail, farmers farm, and astronauts routinely blast into an inhospitable cosmos. Whether they are motivated by the promise of adventure, romance, or the need to earn an honest living, they are determined, exhilarated, and always longing for a safe return.

Like every kind of explorer, we all crave both safety and adventure and are never in a better position to appreciate both than when we play or work on the boundary between different realms of experience. With his customary eloquence and honesty, John Updike wrote that one of the most pleasant experiences of his childhood was to huddle warm and dry beneath an overturned chair on the front porch while a steady summer rain fell just beyond his reach. To be out of danger, but only just, is a situation that many of us can appreciate as when we sit by a cozy fire watching a snowstorm rage outside our window.

Boundaries and borders with their unique opportunities for safety and adventure are not limited to the physical world but mark the landscape of our interior lives as well. The margin between fantasy and reality can be a playground for the artist, a battleground for someone in the throes of psychosis, and an observation platform for anyone contemplating the future through the eyes of imagination.

Psychology has a long tradition of respect for the concept of boundaries and borders. Stimulus barriers, thresholds of awareness, and developmental stages are some of our better-known ways to describe changes in our manner of experiencing the world. We cross some of these lines many times in the course of a single day and others more slowly at periods of significant change over a lifetime. Now, somewhere between a day and a lifetime, we have a season, a few short months of summer to cross the frontier between the commonplace and the exotic, a summer to celebrate life on the edge.

From *New England Psychologist*, July 2006.

• • •

TRUTH, LOVE, AND UNCERTAINTY

As the country gears up for another presidential campaign and candidates place their stories before the American public, we will be listening for themes that resonate with our own experience. Politicians count on this resonance and are masters of the art of presenting themselves in a way that will strike a responsive chord in the minds and hearts of the greatest number of citizens. Party lines, political philosophies, and social and ethical positions on everything from

reproductive issues to foreign policy will be dusted off, highly pol-
ished, and put on display for all to admire and endorse in the privacy
of the voting booth.

Unfortunately, there is usually little nuance in the pronounce-
ments of candidates for office. Republicans are expected to be conser-
vative; Democrats, liberal; and Independents, usually associated with
a single good idea like protecting the consumer or the environment.

If a candidate dares to consider publicly the costs as well as the
benefits of the party line, he or she is accused of being either disloyal
or, perhaps even worse, indecisive. As frustrating as this situation
may be for some, it is actually quite consistent with the way many
of us live our lives. We like name brands. We trust that Kleenex will
deliver a better facial tissue than Brand X, and if both companies
come up with the same good improvement, we are more likely to buy
"The New Improved Kleenex" than "The New Improved Brand X."

We are vulnerable not only to the attraction of recognized brands
but also to the belief that one brand is better than the other because
it is completely different, sometimes its polar opposite. This dynamic
is not exclusive to the political scene nor are psychologists immune to
the follies of the human condition just because we happen to make
it our area of study.

In the setting where I practice, we have our own variation of the
liberal/conservative polarity in the way different staff interpret and
enforce hospital policy, in our ongoing dialogue between the interests
of patient rights and community responsibility, and in the scores of
decisions that we make every day about how to respond to people
who need structure as well as understanding.

Consider the woman who tells the group that she believes a patient
from another part of the hospital has been coming to her unit and

directing her peers to "do bad things" to her. In response to her disclosure, an equally paranoid man leaves the room and, after a few minutes, returns to ask if the group was talking about him when he was gone.

Assured that he was not the subject of conversation, he takes his seat as another group member asks if she is the suspected culprit and, if not, is it anyone else in the room. The original speaker identifies a heretofore silent peer who protests her innocence. Now group members begin to take sides, some supporting the accuser, others coming to the defense of the accused.

The therapist does not have the choice of providing structure or understanding because both are clearly needed. While empathy calls for an acknowledgement of the vulnerability that several of the group members are feeling, reality clamors for equal time. Enter psychoeducation and an attempt to explain that paranoid thinking is a common symptom of serious mental illness making its appearance among us even as we try to identify and define it. If group members have enough trust and goodwill for the group leaders and one another, some of them may listen to the alternate explanation for their paranoid assumptions.

Over time, one or two may even come to entertain the possibility that the alternate explanation is correct.

The twentieth-century philosopher Edith Stein concluded that love and truth are inseparable. Her work admonishes us neither to accept anything as truth that does not contain love nor to accept anything as love that does not contain truth. Stein's writings on empathy challenge us to understand not only the content of our patients' experience but also the experience of their content. It is not enough to know what the paranoid person thinks, but we must also be able to acknowledge how he or she feels.

As psychologists, we are not above falling prey to the polarized thinking of political ideologies, religious dogma, clinical theories, or individual preferences for a tough or tender approach in our dealings with others.

We may slip into believing that our way of assessing a situation is the only correct interpretation, think that we can dispense unconditional love without sometimes hard truths, or proclaim the truth without regard to its impact on the listener. We do this because we value our education and experience, we want to be helpful, and we know what is right for our patients. To think otherwise is to give up the same kind of certainty that tempts us to buy the brand name or vote the party line. To think otherwise is to admit the possibility that the solutions to our patients' dilemmas are not always clear and that the beginning of change is an uncertainty that we are called upon to share.

From *New England Psychologist*, April 2007.

• • •

WHAT I DIDN'T GET
FOR THE HOLIDAYS

This is a story that began forty years ago. When I was just starting out in psychology, it all seemed so complicated that I was never quite sure I knew what I was doing. Then one night an old man appeared to me in a dream. He held a large diamond-shaped crystal that he described as the crystal of wisdom. I did what any resourceful but insecure beginner would do in that kind of situation. I asked him to give me the crystal. That's exactly what I need. May I have it? Not so fast, the old man replied, I'm blankety blank years old, and this crystal is all I have left. You're young and at the peak of health. You have your whole life ahead of you. By the time you are my age, you'll have your own crystal.

I never forgot that dream, and from time to time, I wondered how the crystal would arrive when I turned blankety blank. I hit that milestone during this holiday season, and I am still waiting. The crystal was not sitting on my bedside table when I awoke on my birthday. Nor was it on my breakfast plate, or in the coat closet, on the front seat of my car, or anywhere in my office at the hospital.

Snapping into a more reasonable frame of mind, I realized that the crystal would probably come by FedEx and would be waiting for me when I got home. I was wrong again. So here I am, blankety blank years old, after a joyous holiday season but still without the crystal of wisdom. Just when I had begun to think I had been duped all along, a colleague suggested the obvious. The FedEx people delivered the crystal to the wrong house. Of course, with that simple assumption, everything fell into place, and I had a strategy to recover what my dream visitor so long ago had promised would be rightfully mine.

All I had to do was find the address where the crystal had been delivered, ring the doorbell, say that there must have been some mistake, and ask for it. I would start in my own neighborhood and, if necessary, expand my search from there.

Before I could put my plan into action, my neighbor was knocking on the kitchen door bearing, I imagined, the gift mistakenly delivered to his house. No, he was here to announce his decision to have all the pine trees in his yard taken down. Because his plan would radically alter the appearance of his property and to a certain extent mine, this man was showing his usual consideration that makes him such a good neighbor and friend. Even without a crystal, it takes wisdom to appreciate the possible effects of your actions on others, and once you have done that, then it's equally wise to tell them what to expect.

My neighbor's wisdom in this matter came as no surprise. In the years we have shared a common property line, we have had many yard work conversations about everything from the challenges of family life to speculations about the existence of an afterlife. Although his recent announcement and the reasons for his decision clearly showed wisdom, it was not of the sudden and unexpected variety that one might anticipate if it came from a crystal delivered by FedEx. Besides, he knows the dream and would never hold out on me if the package came to his house instead of mine.

So I kept looking. Perhaps whoever it is that sends these crystals thought it best to have mine delivered to my office. In a big new hospital with labyrinthine corridors and lots of meeting rooms and offices tucked in every available corner, it would be easy to deliver a package to the wrong place. All I had to do was to listen more carefully in all of my conversations with colleagues and patients, and when I heard a sudden increase in wise statements, I would know where to find my crystal.

The more I listened, the more wisdom I heard, but it rarely came packaged and ready for instant use. The ideas had to be weighed and tested against the challenges of everyday life before they took on the heft of true wisdom.

When I listened to patients struggling to find new meaning in lives shattered by misfortune, mental illness, or their own rash behavior, I entered into a dialogue not unlike that of any two people looking for answers to big questions. When everything you counted on is lost, how do you make a meaningful life out of what remains? How do you take responsibility for the hurt you have caused others and still find a way to forgive yourself? Why do some of us survive the same calamities that destroy others?

Although the circumstances and rules governing the interaction would be different, this conversation is the kind I might have with my neighbor when we take a break from raking leaves. I can image Plato and Aristotle discussing similarly weighty matters over their own back fence though, being revered philosophers, at a much deeper level.

We are all looking for wisdom, and we find it everywhere and nowhere. I have not given up looking for my missing crystal though I suspect it will be less like a beacon and more like myriad glints of light reflected from the surfaces of one broken dream after another. Only by looking closely will I ever know for sure.

Adapted from *New England Psychologist*, January 2013.

• • •

LEARNING TO TRUST THE PROCESS

The interviews are over, the rankings have been submitted, and the cloud has delivered the names of our interns for the next training year. All of that is done, but I am still thinking about an answer one of our applicants gave to my standard question about how he imagined his unique strengths and challenges would influence his performance in our program. After explaining what made him the ideal candidate for the position, he said simply that he was still learning to trust the process. He was talking about the process of psychotherapy, but I am thinking about that and something more.

Doing psychotherapy is not easy. Two people sit together in a room, the patient looking for a way to relieve distress and the therapist applying the principles of psychological science in an artful way to bring about the desired change.

Every encounter combines known and unknown elements, from the initial greetings to the opening silence, the first words spoken by the patient, his subsequent train of associations, and the carefully considered response of the therapist at every juncture of the inter-action. Depending on when and where you went to graduate school and where you did your clinical training, you were taught to look at psychotherapy through the lenses of different theoretical orientations.

In my generation, the psychodynamic orientation predominated, and we learned to pay attention to behavioral manifestations of pre-conscious or unconscious thoughts, wishes, feelings, and impulses. When the interplay of id, ego, and superego generated intrapsychic conflict, insight or self-understanding became the key to solving the resulting problems in living. Ego psychology taught us to respect and encourage the individual's striving for active mastery. Relational theories highlighted the importance of early interactions with attachment figures in developing a healthy sense of self.

Today, the conduct of psychotherapy owes more to cognitive behav-ioral models of the person and methodologies for promoting change with Dialectical Behavior Therapy or DBT as a prime example. Evi-dence-based techniques abound, and our procedures are becoming more clearly focused on specific diagnostic entities or symptom clusters. We have Cognitive Restructuring for Post-Traumatic Stress Disorder, Cognitive Behavior Therapy for Psychosis, Motivational Interviewing to promote behavior change, and a host of other techniques, each with its own prescribed way of doing psychotherapy.

As useful as our expanded toolbox may be, we still begin with two people in a room and a silence hanging heavily between them. How do we treat the silence? Is it something to tolerate as an unavoidable delay or appreciate as the matrix of creative change? I remember a personable young man with schizophrenia who never tired of telling me how fascinated he was with psychology and asking me what he should talk about in our therapy sessions.

To discourage his habit of filling my voicemail with random thoughts, I suggested he write down what he wanted to tell me. The unintended consequence of my brilliant suggestion was a laundry list of topics that he proceeded to read one by one in our therapy sessions after first asking in what order he should read them.

One day, he was caught in a rainstorm on the way to the office, and his list all but disintegrated. He salvaged what he could in a paper bag and pulled out one scrap at a time to read me its contents. Forget the list, I said, and just speak your thoughts. The mind has a way of finding words for what is most important. He looked at me skeptically but took my advice. The process was already at work.

It is not easy to trust the process of doing psychotherapy or, for that matter, any process over which we do not have complete control. We have a carefully worked out procedure for selecting interns and trainees, complete with multiple readers for every application, key variables to track and rate during interviews, and a final group discussion of each candidate's strengths and areas for development.

Before the meeting begins, I have a good idea of where I stand on the applicants I interviewed, but I did not see them all. I trust my colleagues as they trust me. Two hours later we emerge with a decision that always feels right. The procedure makes it possible, but the process makes it happen.

It is an axiom of the scientific method that the more we know about every variable that influences an outcome, the better able we will be to produce the results we desire. I couldn't arrange for my patient to get caught in a rainstorm, but at least I learned from it. And let's not forget those unconscious processes that shake us out of our routine ways of thinking and produce surprising results. Descartes is said to have invented analytical geometry in a vision, and Stephen King once explained that the "boys in the basement" write his novels.

There are times in every life when we can't imagine a good outcome from our current circumstances or even conceive of the possibility that we will survive. Loss of a loved one, our health, a job, or our place in the world can change everything. Even the necessary changes that come with new stages in life, offering exciting possibilities and unknown dangers, can fill us with anxiety. The next time someone tells me they are learning to trust the process, I will simply answer, so am I.

From *New England Psychologist*, March 2015.